Another Nip Around The World

MALCOLM GREENWOOD

FOREWORD BY WALLACE MILROY

D1477247

NEIL WILSON PUBLISHING
GLASGOW · SCOTLAND

Published by Neil Wilson Publishing Ltd
303a The Pentagon Centre
36 Washington Street
GLASGOW
G3 8AZ
Tel: 0141-221-1117
Fax: 0141-221-5363
E-mail: nwp@cqm.co.uk
http://www.nwp.co.uk/

© Malcolm Greenwood, 1997

The author has established his moral right to be identified as the author
of this work
A catalogue record for this book is available from the British Library.

ISBN 1-897784-69-4
Typeset in Times
Designed by Janene Reid
Printed by WSOY, Finland

Contents

Acknowledgements

F irst and foremost I would like to thank the sponsors whose credentials can be found at the rear of the book and without whose help this project would not have been possible. However in the course of writing I would sincerely like to thank the following people.

CANADA	Ian & John Hanna, Toronto
	Jim O'Carroll, Halifax, Nova Scotia
ENGLAND	Jack and Wallace Milroy, London
	Alison Dillon & David Steele, London
FINLAND	Tuula Korhonen, Helsinki
FRANCE	Mark Allen, Beaune
	Jean-Pierre Got, Bordeaux
HOLLAND	Annelies Bink, Amsterdam
ITALY	Antony Zanussi, Pordenone
	Cristina Calasso, Milan
NORWAY	Arve Røys Stranden, Oslo
SCOTLAND	Mario Cabrelli, Barry & Helen Chown, Gordon Webster, John Nicholson and Dorothy Allan, Elgin
	George & John Grant, Glenfarclas
	Linda McAdam & Andy McBean, Moray College, Elgin
	Norman Shepherd & Allan Mearns, Aberdeen
	Dorothy Brandie, Craigellachie
	Bruce Williams, Glasgow

SWEDEN   Jonas Wahlman, Stockholm
              Alan Watson, Stockholm
              Kristian Rankloo, Malmo

I would like to express my appreciation to the two artists who collaborated on this book. They are Erik Foseid of Stockholm who has illustrated the opening chapter and Grahame Nairn of Moray College, Elgin.

MALCOLM GREENWOOD, ELGIN
SEPTEMBER 1997

Foreword

Malcolm Greenwood and I have known each other for several years and I am delighted to see him join the inner circle of whisky lovers who have turned authors. I wish him every success with *Another Nip Around The World*. It is a sign of the high regard in which Malcolm is held that this book has attracted so many sponsors.

As a reader you can look forward to an entertaining few evenings, dram in hand, as Malcolm takes you with him around Europe on some of his many sales trips. Needless to say, they almost all have three things in common: good company, good food and fine drink.

But what strikes me most about Malcolm's escapades is his willingness to allow us to be part of them. He has no airs and graces, no pretensions or prejudices . . . what you see is what you get, even when it looks as though the poor, misguided fool is falling in love!

The fact that Malcolm's stories are so often humorous speaks volumes for the type of character he attracts in his working life. He rarely returns to Glenfarclas without a story to tell or without a tale that has been told to him over the rim of a whisky glass in the corner of an atmospheric bar somewhere in Europe.

And how he enjoys his food. The loneliness of the long distance whisky salesman has never afflicted Malcolm whose taste in cuisine is as gregarious and outward-going as his personality. There appears to be no limit to what Malcolm is prepared to eat in his search for greater knowledge in the restaurants, bistros and bars of the world, and we share in his pleasure.

So pour a dram, settle back into your best armchair and let Malcolm take you for *Another Nip Around The World*.

WALLACE MILROY, LONDON
SEPTEMBER 1997

The Scots Hogmanay

What makes Scotland so charming is the sociability so evident during what I call the 'funny season'. Old neighbourly squabbles are buried, or at least temporarily forgotten, young and old mix, strangers are welcomed, and in effect a street party atmosphere develops which can last for days. The pubs shut and people's homes open. The biggest street party in the world at this time occurs on Princes Street, Edinburgh, and in the Highlands the atmosphere is no less rewarding.

After the 'bells', the stroke of midnight on New Year's Eve, it is traditional (and supposedly lucky) for a tall dark-haired man to 'first foot' his friends, that is to be the first person over the doorstep in the New Year.

This is the tale of Jake Longman who decided to carry out this tradition after he had consumed pint after pint of ale and dram after dram of whisky since the early afternoon. Jake Longman decided to first foot Laurie, a local journalist and his wife Moira. She had been hard at work all day, making preparations for the biggest night in the Scots calendar.

Jake is a master coppersmith who crafts distilling equipment by day. Built like a Victorian lavatory, he has hands that resemble baseball gloves and a face that only a mother could love. He could, however, cleverly fashion copper as easily as children fashion clay. This metal was favoured by early illicit distillers for its malleability and this has continued into the modern 'legal' distilling industry.

The party was in full swing when he arrived, the open fire banked high with glowing coals. In his pocket he carried a full

JAN
FEB
MAR
APR
MAY
JUNE
JULY
AUG
SEPT
OCT
NOV
DEC

1

bottle of whisky which brushed shoulders with a lump of coal, a symbol of good fortune, meaning 'lang may yer lum reek' (long may your chimney smoke).

In this case there was plenty of smoke, fire and heat. The wall of warmth and hot bodies which greeted Jake engulfed and consumed him. He immediately regretted having eaten a black pudding supper (or was it that last double whisky?) He teetered and swayed as smiling rosy faces offered savouries, cocktail sausages, pickles and cheese. His enormous jowls slowly turned grey and like some distillery chimney on the point of demolition, he swayed at an impossible angle and began his inevitable descent. The entire Hogmanay buffet, magnificently laid out on a huge glass-topped table, lay in his downward path.

CRASH! Jake was unceremoniously dragged outside and laid out on the pavement, like some mediaeval knight on a stone crypt.

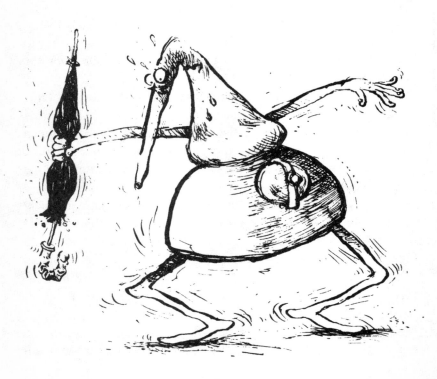

NON OBLIGATORY LUMP OF COAL

The night was frosty but fair and it was decided that he would be checked regularly — besides no one had the strength to drag him any farther!

It is not always easy to understand why the Scots have such a voracious appetite for liquor compared to their English and European neighbours. Perhaps the influence of Celtic ancestry, the harsh climate and a need to appear manly and virile have contributed to these characteristics.

Recently, to escape a Scottish Hogmanay for my liver's sake, I headed to Ireland, to the west-coast town of Galway, to be sure. Big mistake. If you like fat and fleshy prawns, clams and oysters, this is the place to visit. But for a diet and some leisurely detoxification — forget it!

The Irish, I was about to learn, take New Year's celebrations very seriously, even by Scottish standards. The pubs are charming, and almost all of them offer folk, fiddle or harp music. Men, women, children, the old and young alike are encouraged to mix.

JAN
FEB
MAR
APR
MAY
JUNE
JULY
AUG
SEPT
OCT
NOV
DEC

I soon discovered and savoured some of their lesser-known Irish whiskeys like Ballygeary and Connemara; toddies with cloves and lemons re-affirmed my opinion of them — they were delicious and I didn't even have a cold! Irish coffee was wonderful and the Guinness . . . well I have never tasted its like before — creamy, rich and velvety soft. One could not fail to be impressed by the careful pouring technique which resembled the Bavarian style — a little and often. Curiously, some of the pubs are inter-connected with others by side doors and passages, removing the need to venture outdoors at all!

The Celtic breakfasts served to me in Galway were fit for road builders. Two fried eggs with fat spicy sausages, black pudding, potato scones, tomatoes, baked beans, mushrooms and fried bread accompanied by a pint of dark milky Guinness followed by dense Irish soda breads, which were so rich and heavy that standing up afterwards was a feat in itself.

On a lesser note, I remember trying my first skiing lesson high up in the Swiss Alps in Grindelwald on New Year's Day. My head pounded from the previous night's celebrations and I had forgotten to take my sunglasses. My German-speaking instructor became quite exasperated with me after a short while. Half an hour was enough. Soaked, frustrated and cold, the lure of the nearby aprés-ski chalet was irresistible .

'You steel have af an hoar', the instructor insisted. 'I weel make you ski', he commanded.

Oh no you won't, I thought. 'Fancy a beer, Hans?'

He shrugged and miserably gave up on me. New Year's Day was only for skiing in these parts.

Similarly Long Island, New York was equally disappointing. Sitting with my brother in Billie's Bar in Port Jefferson, the 'bells' tolled, fancy hats were passed around, a few hands shaken, then it was back to business as usual, with everyone departing home an hour later.

No, a Celtic Hogmanay takes some beating, and we Scots then have a three-week run into another fine Scots invention . . . the Burns suppers! This is a wonderful custom and has to be seen to be believed. This annual event held on January 25th celebrates our national bard Robert Burns. It is perhaps curious that there is no tradition of celebrating Shakespeare's birthday or other famous

JAN
FEB
MAR
APR
MAY
JUNE
JULY
AUG
SEPT
OCT
NOV
DEC

literary, artistic or musical talents. There are no Dumas dinners, Picasso lunches or Bach breakfasts. But all around the globe people gather to acclaim the poetry of Burns and drink to his immortal memory.

HAGGIS WITH DETONATOR AND TIME FUSE

They also make a very welcome post-Hogmanay blues antidote. Winter is at its bleakest and the pretty snows of Christmas have turned to slush. Dark, bitterly cold nights will persist into April. I often think that a party should be held at the end of February as well, thus breaking up the long winter. By the end of January Scottish mirth, song, food and drink need rejuvenation and a Burns Supper is a great excuse.

THE BLACK PUDDING

The 'supper' is not unlike the 'Celtic' breakfast. Haggis, mashed potato and turnip (neeps) act like blotting paper and are guaranteed to stall even the most enthusiastic raconteur's thirst. Digestion is aided by fine malt scotch whisky.

February will be easier on the liver, I ponder, as I worry about January's daily intake levels and begin a record of daily units. My doctor would have a coronary if he saw my notes!

Perhaps I should have finished that skiing lesson!

Cool Nuns Down Mexico Way

In 1925, a small printer in Mainz, Germany was asked to design a modern and picturesque label to replace the house label that Sichel wines had been using for over 60 years. They came up with a picture of nuns gathering grapes and a legend was started . . .

Blue Nun Liebfraumilch can justly claim to be the world's most famous wine. Its meteoric growth during the sixties and seventies made it into a household name. Sweet and fruity, easily drunk and with a pronounceable name, its success seemed secured.

One of our past distributors in the UK, until 1993, was an offshoot of this company, H Sichel and Sons Ltd, 4 York Buildings, Adelphi, London. A stone's throw away from the Savoy Hotel, their main office was a venerable rabbit warren just off Adam Street. Indeed, 'Adam' architectural features were very evident in the building, including the stairways and intricate fire surrounds. It was a ruinously expensive location in the heart of London, but it oozed atmosphere. The most memorable place, however, must have been the tasting room, where many staff accumulated after work, presumably to miss the rush hour! In the centre of this room was the most enormous spittoon I have ever seen. Made out of white porcelain, it looked like a small bath. I learned later that it had actually been procured from a Welsh coal mine, where the miners, bared to the waist, would scrub up after a grimy shift underground.

The marketing director for Sichel at the time, was David

JAN
FEB
MAR
APR
MAY
JUNE
JULY
AUG
SEPT
OCT
NOV
DEC

7

Steele. Known as 'Steely', he was a tough, burly, terrier-like Yorkshireman; good-humoured and enthusiastic. He had white aristocratic hair, a ruddy complexion, double chin and dark twinkly eyes. We hit it off from the start and after meeting his wife Sue, we all found that we shared a distinctly similar sense of humour. It was always a treat to visit Sichel in London, and after our meetings David and Sue often invited me out to dinner afterwards. These were memorable events.

David's brand manager, Alison Dillon, was a dedicated marketeer. Had the company survived I am sure that many of the agency brands would have gone from strength to strength under their management. The main brand, Blue Nun was fighting a price war with its arch rival Black Tower, the battleground being the multiple supermarkets, where margins are slim even at the best of times. On the demand side consumers were becoming more and more discerning and moving up market. New World wines, which were inexpensive and of good quality, were making huge inroads. Coupled to this the central London office, large sales force, high overheads and low margins proved to be insurmountable problems.

Ironically, the most profitable area was not their core business but the agency products they represented. Great names such as the Torres wines from Spain, Hill Smith of Australia, Wente of California, Noval Port from Portugal and Glenfarclas malt whisky of Scotland were invaluable earners.

I maintain, and this benefits from hindsight, that if this profitable area had been fully recognised and developed further, the office sold and the company relocated outside London, then it may have survived and prospered. Many of the sales staff went on to greater things, but it was a great shame that this arm of the Sichel company went down the tube. That aside, it is with great fondness that I remember the 'Sichel' days and my time spent with David.

He worked hard, but also played hard. He had a huge appetite, and introduced me to some wonderful and not so wonderful cuisine! David and Sue had a passion for real Chinese food, and

after work we often headed to nearby Chinatown. The Lee Ho Fook in Gerrard Street to be exact, stuffed with dining Chinese clientele, a good endorsement for a classic Chinese restaurant. I was presented with crispy aromatic duck, served with wafer-thin pancakes spread with Hoi Sin sauce and sprinkled with thinly sliced cucumber and shredded spring onion, all washed down with hot rice wine — delicious! Don't look for chic adornments here, the restaurant is clean and functional, the food authentic and affordable — this is a definite favourite of mine.

Different in style yet equally wonderful is another gem, Down Mexico Way with Spanish influences at 25 Swallow Street, connecting Piccadilly with Regent Street. The restaurant sports the largest collection of Andalucian ceramic tiles outside Spain, and the walls are adorned with them. A fountain trickles gently away among abundant lush greenery and melancholic Latin music plays unobtrusively in the background. This creates a cool relaxed atmosphere, at odds with what we were about to eat.

David chose the starters for us all and in so doing revealed his wicked sense of humour. He knew I would be visiting the drinks buyer at Harrods the following morning and he had plans for me. His choice was the Chilli Crab soup. On arriving it did not look sinister at all — quite the reverse in its blushing pink innocent hues. But it was shockingly hot going down and was to prove a real bum scorcher the next day when I inwardly cursed 'that bastard' Steele as I wriggled in agony in the hot seat at Harrods! The main course, thankfully, was much cooler — Fajitas filled with chicken, smoked over mesquite wood, served on a sizzling skillet with peppers and onions, accompanied with flour tortillas, sour cream, guacamole, refried black beans, and ice-cold Sol beer. The fire in my mouth was nearly extinguished, but the heat was spreading, downwards and downwards, to hell!

Down Mexico Way is yet another sensibly priced retreat in central London, and if you can avoid the Crab soup, or as I call it 'Rodrigo's Revenge', you can survive.

Talking of revenge, when the dust had settled on Sichel's demise, I invited Alison Dillon out for a 'farewell' dinner, during which we both got rather tipsy. In the conversation I boldly asked her outright what her most embarrassing experience had been? Funnily enough, she explained, this had occurred quite recently and she turned a shade pinker in the process, telling me that it involved David. 'Go on', I encouraged her.

The story began when she had been working late one evening and on passing David's office door was greeted by the sounds of unusual grunts and moans coming from within. On returning from a 'scrubbing down' after work in the tasting room, David had relaxed on his tilted chair, feet up on his desk. He eventually nodded off, but in doing so his chair had passed the angle of no return. When it overturned it wedged itself and Steely firmly between a filing cabinet and fax machine. Only two tremulous legs could be seen waving in the air when Alison opened the door. No harm was done, except to his pride, and Alison was sworn to secrecy.

The following morning she could not contain herself and told her story to the telesales people in the basement. When David walked in there was an explosion of laughter.

'My, my, what jolly people! Oh Alison could I have a word with you?' he asked. Her face went crimson, certain in the knowledge he had overheard every gory detail. She felt like a traitor, a Judas and wished she could disappear. On ascending the stairs she decided to apologise wholeheartedly.

'David, I'm so sorry, you must have heard it all, but it was such a funny, er, amusing incident, I could not resist telling the crew downstairs, I'm truly sorry', she implored him.

'Don't worry my dear', he replied, 'it was a funny predicament, don't blame yourself!' Alison was clearly relieved.

'By the way,' he enquired, 'are you free to go up to Scotland

JAN
FEB
MAR
APR
MAY
JUNE
JULY
AUG
SEPT
OCT
NOV
DEC

next Wednesday?'

'Why yes', she replied.

'Oh good', acknowledged David. 'That's all I think. Oh, one last thing Alison . . . ', he continued.

'Yes', she replied.

' . . . regarding your little conversation downstairs. I didn't hear a word of it!'

Thrills, Stills and Hot Pants

I was looking forward to this ten-day trip which would include Norway, Sweden, Finland and Denmark. Since Sweden and Finland joined the EU the Government monopolies on purchasing, distribution and retailing liquor are breaking up. This will allow for fairer competition from other countries, and means that whisky prices should drop. Norway put a spanner in the works by voting 'no' to EU membership, while wishing closer associated status, so the monopoly situation is being segmented to allow some degree of competition. I am filled with a feeling of curiosity and interest in this new era.

I have collected a few facts about Norway on my travels:

1. The famous maniacal 'scream' painting by Munch hangs in Oslo.
2. Norway has the highest sugar and yeast purchasing trends in the world. This is not in the pursuit of 'home baking' but 'home distilling' where this is a national hobby.
3. Norway has a breathtakingly daunting geography and as Norwegians will invariably and proudly relate, if the country is

JAN
FEB
MAR
APR
MAY
JUNE
JULY
AUG
SEPT
OCT
NOV
DEC

turned upside down from the Oslo axis, its tip would touch Rome.

4. They have a strange love for long-nosed trolls.
5. As Vikings they pillaged Scotland, but failed to introduce home-distilling?
6. The Northern Lights (*aurora borealis*) can indeed be seen in the light of the morning. This is a direct result of being engrossed in the 'national hobby' the previous evening.
7. They recently won the Eurovision Song Contest and admit to it!

The last time I had been in Norway was in 1979, returning to Bergen from the Brent oil field. For almost four years I worked this routine, two weeks on and two weeks off and I have many fond memories of that time. The tours on the oil rig consisted of hard work and good hearty food, the cuisine being a mixture of English and Norwegian. Nouvelle cuisine would never have caught on, it was more in the Desperate-Dan-cow-pie-with-horns style, and it was the first time I had eaten moose and smoked reindeer. There was no alcohol or women and generally there were no problems. It was, however, a bit boring at times.

The crew operating the rig I was on were all Norwegian. My first impression of these people was disappointing. They appeared to be arrogant and aloof. I did not realise at first, being only 21, that this was a mixture of shyness, caution and good manners. In fact once you got to know them, over the weeks and months, they turned out to be the most genuine of people. They, like the Scots, and especially those living further north, display a cautious suspicion of strangers. The effect of this has been likened to a ketchup bottle — you do not get much to start with, but then it comes out in a hearty rush.

Alcohol was strictly forbidden on these rigs, but this rule tended to be broken. One trick was to carry on board a small bag of oranges. Innocent enough one might suppose. That is until you cut the top off, suck hard, and you have a ready-made screwdriver or vodka cocktail. You do need to know a pretty nurse back home though, one who has access to clean hypodermic syringes.

So here I was about to embark on the Color-Line ferry service from Newcastle to Stavanger, in March. The weather in the North Sea at this time of year can be quite atrocious, but I have reasonable sea legs and this vessel would not be dry! I boarded at Newcastle docks at 18.30 hours with a little trepidation and went in search of my cabin which was to be in the bowels of the boat, next to the car deck. It was hot and stuffy, but at least I could see out. The Tannoy kept reminding passengers not to use the lifts in an emergency and my cabin was six floors below open deck! The crossing was decidedly rough and many of my fellow passengers experienced what the Americans call 'motion discomfort'.

Watching the news the next morning on Norwegian TV the first feature was of John Major in Parliament. Then came a shot of a deranged and distressed cow. Obviously Norwegians take this very seriously as this was the principal news. The beef and sheep offal scare has made me consider my good friend Mr Haggis. How will he fair I wonder? Perhaps face extinction like his sausage cousins? I hope not, but I can see the product going more up-market. With the Scots love for hot and spicy food perhaps we will see a Raj influence. Our national dish may eventually become a 'Sheek Haggi Kebab'! I wonder what Rabbie would have said of that?

Arriving at a very damp and drizzly Stavanger I was momentarily uplifted on driving on to the motorway bypass. This was short-lived however as it quickly dwindled to a single trunk road and this would be the view through the windscreen for the next 300 miles. The roads twisted and climbed through a wilderness of frozen lakes and heavy snow showers as the freight lorries set the pace. A frustrating and somewhat depressing eight

JAN

FEB

MAR

APR

MAY

JUNE

JULY

AUG

SEPT

OCT

NOV

DEC

hours was spent behind the wheel. The car seemed to entomb me and I left it gladly on arriving in Oslo.

Having asked our agent there to book me into a 'middle range' hotel, I was slightly bemused by the rich ambience of the Hotel Bristol. The hotel porter offered to park my car, which I declined. He did, however, accompany me to the car park as I had many whisky samples to take inside. The porter was anxious to tell me that Mikhail Gorbachev had stayed in the hotel the previous evening. This information raised some concern about the 'middle range' room rate, but it was too late to worry about it. I was going nowhere that night.

The next morning I was met by the very large Arve Røys. He was a good eight inches taller than me, bearded, blue-eyed and built like the proverbial brick house. I thought he appeared a little agitated, and at first put this down to Norwegian shyness, but later learned his infant daughter of 14 months had taken a hard tumble that morning so I could understand his distress. Also his car had been stolen the day before: unbelievably, this is very common in Norway. The cars usually end up in Russia through the back door via Finland. I wonder how Gorbachev got home!

Nevertheless Arve made me most welcome in Oslo and between business exchanges he pointed out places of interest; among them the Nobel Building where they decide on the peace prize each year and a beautiful fairy castle-like parliament house where the Gestapo had their headquarters in the Second World War. Arve explained that an RAF Mosquito flew over the North Sea to bomb it but missed.

Oslo has a pretty harbour and many colourful tram cars. In the evening the bars and restaurants are alive with custom and the choice is international, including Japanese, Mexican, Indian and Thai cuisine.

I chose a traditional Norwegian restaurant despite its name (Mona Lisa) which was recommended by Arve. He was excused from duty due to his mitigating domestic circumstances. I was greeted warmly at the door and, wishing to write a letter, asked for a quiet table. This was dutifully done and the menu arrived swiftly afterwards. The restaurant was 'middle range' and was half-full on a Thursday evening. It was traditional in style with colourful drapes, dark solid furniture, chandeliers and gilt mirrors. A pleasant hubbub was evident and the atmosphere relaxing. Wholesome warm bread with nuts arrived, accompanied by salted butter gently laced with garlic and herbs.

My starter, gravadlax with salad, whetted the appetite. Marinaded medallions of reindeer were irresistible as a main course. This dish was presented in nouvelle cuisine style with the pink meat placed centrally on a cream sauce with a colourful array of baby corn, morels and mangetout. Under the meat a celery and leak mash was hidden. A scooped-out passion fruit contained a cranberry sauce which brilliantly offset the gamyness of the meat with its tartness.

The dinner was reasonably priced at £17 for the generous portions. I felt well-fed, content and ready for a dram. The wine however was outrageously priced. A bottle of Chianti Ruffino 1994 was £24.95, more than double the average restaurant price. I chose a half bottle at a scandalous £14. Hopefully Norway will soon enjoy sensibly priced wines and spirits when it becomes more influenced by the EU.

This, thankfully, would be an early night as I faced another long eight-hour drive the next day to Stockholm for a meeting at 16.00 hours and then a whisky tasting in Upsalla, north of the Stockholm in the evening. Asking for a malt whisky with my coffee I was offered a Jack Daniels! They had only one malt so I chose a deluxe blend. This was priced at £6 for a 4cl measure and again I wondered about those illicit stills!

The espresso coffee was the best deal however, served in proper cups, not the normal thimbles with those ridiculous lugs which the average person cannot grip. It was clear to see that this was Viking country!

Heaven greeted me the next day in the form of the Swedish roads. What bliss! With a 350-mile journey ahead I left early at 06.30 hours.

The sun was shining as I headed towards Stockholm. Swedish

JAN
FEB
MAR
APR
MAY
JUNE
JULY
AUG
SEPT
OCT
NOV
DEC

road systems are Germanic in style, not allowing nature to take the initiative. They were long, wide and straight with gentle curves. Visibility was excellent for overtaking. They had the added feature of hard shoulders or narrow lanes to either side, so it was almost a motorway. These lanes allow freight and agricultural vehicles to pull over without slowing others down thus allowing cars to pass safely without crossing the centre line. Frustration is practically eliminated and safe cruising speeds can be maintained. Scottish road builders should take note, after all John McAdam, a Scot, pioneered modern road building in the nineteenth century.

Stockholm was freezing on arrival and wet snow fell on the streets. Volvos and Saabs naturally dominated the busy streets. The murky weather kept me close to the hotel. Today was Saturday, a partial day off, until I was to meet our distributor in the evening. I spent my free time in search of a wine and spirits shop to see what was on the market. These are called *Systembolagets*, run by the state monopoly and are closed on Saturday! I can think of a few places where this phenomenon would cause a riot. Never mind, I am told all this is soon to change.

The shopping malls here were like any other, with Tie-rack, Laura Ashley, United Colours of Benetton and Macdonalds. The Big Mac tasted like any other. Malls are now a feature all over Europe, the USA and the Far East offering standard styles and products with no obvious cultural or national traits. I soon tired of this, so I went in search of a traditional Swedish pub and found an Irish one instead! A pint of Kilkenny stout went down well, but set me back £4.80. I was intrigued by the condom machine in the gents, which offered you an alcohol breath test device as well. That's what I call safe sex!

Jonas Wahlman, our distributor, picked me up at my hotel in the early evening. As I climbed into his Japanese car he enquired whether or not I would like my 'tush warmer' on or off?

'Tush warmer?' I responded. He was referring to the heated seats. Now I do know that Saab and Volvo pioneered these

JAN
FEB
MAR
APR
MAY
JUNE
JULY
AUG
SEPT
OCT
NOV
DEC

19

systems many years ago, but I explained that I did not realise that other makes of car now incorporated them. As if on cue, Jonas related what must have been one of his favourite 'knock the Brits' stories.

The anecdote concerned a British diplomat's wife on her first visit to Sweden in the sixties. On departing the embassy on a bitterly cold night, she climbed into the back of the Daimler. At that time a 'tush-warmer' was practically unheard of outside Sweden, but at great expense these devices had been installed into the rear seats of the embassy Daimler. The driver flicked them on and pulled out into the traffic flow. A few moments later the lady in question started to fidget and wriggle, in obvious distress. The driver pondered on the cause of such obvious restlessness and was soon put in the picture when the glass partition slid open.

'Ivan, Ivan, quickly, do you have any tissues?' she nervously enquired. The lady's name has remained a closely guarded secret ever since! A clear case of pampering to the lady's every need perhaps?

The islands of Åland in Finland were our next destination on the Sunday and a six-hour sail on the Viking Line's M/s *Amorella*, an ice-breaking ferry which serves the Baltic. Huge amounts of duty-free are purchased on these boats and the bar was quite busy at 8am.

The day was bright with winter scenes persisting. Icebergs predominated the seascape, which changed further north to mosaics of translucent blue. Arriving in Marieham, a maritime port, we booked into the Park Alandia hotel — a good choice as this boasted the only restaurant and pub open that evening. Marieham is famous for the *Pommern* the only remaining four-masted sailing barge in the world. Built in Glasgow in 1903 for the famous grain trade between Australia and the UK, she has remained in harbour since 1939 and now functions as a museum.

The food that evening was delicious; a herring-roe starter (sailor's caviar) followed by minced pike rissoles with warm apple horseradish as a main course. This was washed down with a tarry Karjala beer at 5.2% alcohol by volume.

They had no malt whisky to offer, so we finished with our own cask-strength 105° proof Glenfarclas, which we also offered to the proprietor. This was well received. The sea air, good food and warming dram relaxed me for a wonderful night's sleep.

On our return journey to Stockholm we almost missed the boat. After boarding the ferry, we stowed our luggage in the lockers and settled down in the lounge, with a beer, waiting for the boat to depart. I glanced out of the porthole and noticed another ferry, the M/s *Mariella*, across the harbour. I casually remarked that in the original itinerary sent to me, that was the name of the boat we were to return home on.

My friend choked on his beer, and the next thing I knew we were racing for the lockers. We had to escape from the ferry via the vehicle ramps as the pedestrian access was already raised for departure. We hurried across the harbour jetty and just caught the ferry before it set sail. Another couple of minutes and we would have been on our way to St Petersburg in Russia instead of Stockholm!

JAN

FEB

MAR

APR

MAY

JUNE

JULY

AUG

SEPT

OCT

NOV

DEC

Before returning home my last whisky tasting was in Malmo. The city is situated across the water from Copenhagen and is very much like Amsterdam on a smaller scale . . . canals, cyclists, little pubs, etc.

Malt whisky is starting to be well received here and after my presentation I was invited to visit some pubs and taste the local hooch. At last, I thought, I might see one of the famous Scandinavian illicit stills. Alas, no.

However, this might have proved safer, because 'slammers' are the rage here. Small hard tot glasses are filled with deadly combinations and taken in one shot. One was called 'perrelis' made with Absolut vodka and Turkish licorice lozenges. Another for people who hate washing up, was called 'kex shots': this was a Spanish cream liqueur in a wafer cup like an ice-cream cone. You knocked the whole thing back, cup and all! Bring me a 105° proof Glenfarclas anytime. No, make that a double!

One final observation I noted was a kind of English/Irish rivalry between the Swedes and Norwegians. The former believe the latter to be vain and stupid (and vice versa). For example, a favourite joke made by 'Swegians' is as follows:

Why do 'Swegians' rush out of their homes during a lightning storm?

They think they're going to get their photographs taken!

Roll-off March, roll-on April.

22

Illicit Rape!

April 16, 1996 marked the 250th anniversary of Culloden, the last battle to take place on British soil. A moorland just east of Inverness was the venue for this infamous Scotland vs England clash. When the young Prince Charles Edward Stuart charmed the Highland chiefs into joining him in a rebellion against the English in 1746, men flocked to his standard. Prior to the battle 'Bonnie Prince Charlie' and his generals stayed in nearby Elgin (at the Thunderton House Hotel to be exact) where the battle plan was discussed in a low wooden-beamed room, still in existence. It was rumoured that a fair amount of claret and whisky was consumed during their deliberations, which may help account for the outcome of the battle.

Today a good friend, Kareen Mackenzie, from the Isle of Lewis is the publican here and whenever I take out overseas visitors, a trip to this pub is usually on the agenda. Kareen recently had two of our German agents up to the 'battle room'. It was lit with only two candles and you could have cut the atmosphere with a knife. I hope the owners develop this historic room, as it is only used for storage at present. That apart, the pub offers a good range of malts and guest beers, so it is one of my favourite haunts.

Back to Culloden. The English were led by the very capable but ruthless Duke of Cumberland. Prince Charles and his devoted clansmen were routed and a bloodbath ensued. Prior to the battle 'Butcher Cumberland' had put out a command that no quarter be given, or, in other words, no prisoners were to be taken alive. Every survivor found on the battlefield was put to the sword.

JAN
FEB
MAR
APR
MAY
JUNE
JULY
AUG
SEPT
OCT
NOV
DEC

Incredibly a flower called 'Sweet William' was later named after him.

Despite a reward on his head of £30,000[1] Prince Charles escaped to France via Skye, never to return. There, he died a drunken wretch and the Scottish Highlands were never the same again.

The Highland Clearances followed which effectively killed off the clan system. Families were forced out of their dwellings by lairds hungry for richer pickings. There were others who would pay higher rents: lowland sheep farmers and tacksmen (sub-tenants) related to their lairds. Subsequently, the hardy Cheviot sheep replaced the people. This resulted in many thousands of Scots emigrating to the new world. In 1772 alone, over 6,000 people left Inverness-shire and Ross to sail to the Americas, and that was only the start . . .

All was not lost however. It was around this time that illicit distillation started to make a headway in the Highlands. Vast and remote sections of the west and north became virtually uninhabited. The only reminders of human existence were the burnt-out shells of crofts and homesteads — some of which can still be seen today. Crude tracks, often inaccessible during the long winters, allowed for almost unchecked distillation.

It has been said that if you can boil a kettle, then you can make whisky. This is an oversimplification, but not far off the mark. You have to be able to brew a crude beer for a start, and Boots the chemist was not around the corner then to supply a home-brewing kit! The choice of cereal was barley or bere as it was then known, the staple of the Highland diet at that time. The apparatus or 'kit' was simple: a crude kettle with a long neck and a coil of hollow copper tubing called a 'worm' and a water-filled wooden tub in which to cool the distillate inside the worm. That was it: a kettle, worm and tub.

Heat was required from below to take the beer to almost boiling point. At this time there was an unlimited amount of peat

[1] Worth £1.5 million at 1997 figures (Source – Bank of Scotland)

24

to burn. The worm was attached to the long neck of the kettle and alcohol vapours from the gently boiling beer condensed to form new spirit called 'spike' or 'clearic' (colourless), which was crude and fiery, distilled only once, but truly 'duty-free'.

This state of affairs was not to last long. As with all good things costing next to nothing, the Government started to take an interest. Squads of customs and excise officers (gaugers) were sent north and many hundreds of illicit stills were seized. Despite this the Highlanders persisted in their practices with even greater vigilance. Lookouts were regularly posted and signals used to warn of the approaching authorities.

The distillery of Cardhu on Speyside has its roots steeped in this illicit practice. Before being legally licensed it was, like others, little more than a farm with a 'secret still'. A red flag was flown above the barn steading when gaugers were in the area.

Around 1810 the local 'brew' in Speyside was widely sought after. It was smuggled through the remote hills on horseback to the coast, then sold in small wooden firkins in Aberdeen, Dundee,

Glasgow and further afield. Over 400 small stills operated in Speyside alone. In one year the excise officers from Elgin made 3,061 discoveries of illicit distilling which was fast becoming a major winter sport! One of the last stills to be seized before 'legal' licenses were issued, was near Dufftown, on the Cabrach moor.

To be charged and convicted of illicit

JAN
FEB
MAR
APR
MAY
JUNE
JULY
AUG
SEPT
OCT
NOV
DEC

whisky making the customs officers actually had to catch you 'in the act'. The 'kit' however was easily dispersed in different directions so it was difficult to catch the culprits 'redhanded'. One of the last to be convicted was caught in possession of the full 'kit', and thus intent was established. The local sheriff on sentencing the poor fellow, enquired if he wished to say anything in his defence.

A silence filled the courtroom. Then suddenly the accused bawled out at the top of his voice, 'Rape!'

'Rape?' enquired the Sheriff, adding, 'Be careful what you say, man, or I'll have you for contempt!'

'Yes . . . rape, my lord!' he exclaimed. 'You might as well charge me with that as well.'

'And why?' questioned the sheriff.

'Because I have all the necessary equipment!'

I started my April entry with the arrival of Prince Charles in Glenfinnan, one of Scotland's most beautiful and desolate settings at the eastern end of Loch Shiel. A simple stone column surmounted by a statue of a highlander stands here; a place where dreams were once conceived only to be so bloodily aborted soon afterwards. Bonnie Prince Charlie is immortalised for his audacity and courage against seemingly incredible odds. He marched his army as far south as Derby and so threatened the English throne. He followed in the footsteps and traditions of William Wallace, Robert the Bruce and other 'bravehearts'.

My reason for being in Glenfinnan (at the Glenfinnan House Hotel) was inspired by passions and dreams. I was there to attend a Highland wedding. I remember most of all the very 'style' of the occasion. Naturally Scottish, country and most of all Highland.

Instead of the normal regal adornments, the bride and groom had chosen a very natural look, which I thought worked wonderfully. The bride's headdress consisted of a modest boater-style straw hat adorned with wild flowers. The church was decorated in the same simple style, with heathers, thistles and ferns. Orchids and roses stood no chance here. Make no mistake, however, this was no hippy or gypsy affair, but just so individual and original that I could not help being affected by the atmosphere. It was understated and very different from the extravagant and expensive affairs currently in vogue.

The church service was held in the west-coast town of Fort William, followed by a reception and ceilidh at the Glenfinnan Hotel. Even in the height of summer, a log fire smouldered in the foyer, looked down upon by numerous stags' heads and other stuffed creatures from a bygone age.

Prior to entering the hotel we were all dutifully assembled on the lawn outside to pose for the dreaded photograph. The organisers had chosen a particularly creative fellow who insisted on having the entire entourage photographed from an elevated position, in this case, a first-floor window looking down on the assembled party.

Most of the men were kilted for the occasion and it being a warm, balmy evening the ladies dared to bare some flesh. The general noise and body scents must have acted like a dinner-gong for our west-coast friend, the midge. The sky darkened as the cloud of insects, like microscopic Transylvanian vampires, hunted down their victims.

'Stand still!' implored the cameraman.

'Fat chance', someone muttered, as the swarm tucked into their aperitifs. The men faired worst of all, particularly the 'real' Scotsmen and we escaped to the hotel bar!

The ceilidh would reach a frenzy after many jigs and other swirling dances. Like a spark from a catherine wheel one poor dervish lost his grip during a whirling eightsome reel and shot into orbit. He crashed spectacularly through a set of French windows to land unceremoniously on top of a rhododendron bush. I do believe that if this individual had been stone cold sober he would have sustained untold injuries. He re-emerged, unscathed, all

JAN
FEB
MAR
APR
MAY
JUNE
JULY
AUG
SEPT
OCT
NOV
DEC

spaniel-eyed, with glass cracking under foot, to be met with hoots of laughter and a glass of whisky shoved into his hand. This is the stuff of Highland weddings!

It was also a memorable day because of a very special encounter I had with 'the Seer Annie' who was gifted with *taibh-searachd* (second sight). She lived on the road from Fort William to Glenfinnan so our small coach party, decided to visit her on the way to the ceilidh.

28

We knocked on the door of the tiny cottage which was opened by a wild-eyed, craggy-faced woman. She must have been at least 90 years old, yet there was a childlike innocence about her, which was pleasing and welcoming. To describe the cottage as tiny would be an understatement; two rooms with low beamed ceilings meant we had to crouch inside and there was no electricity or running water!

A 'kerry-oot' had been bought for the mammoth half-hour journey, so I was able to offer her a wee dram which was warmly received. She added some cold brackish-brown water from a pump outside, then sat back in a tattered moss-green velvet armchair, the seat of which had collapsed many moons ago.

'Tell me', I enquired, 'is it true that you have special skills?'

She smiled warmly and I thought her face was going to crack. 'Sonny', she replied, 'the truth of the matter is, yes. Do not believe that just because your senses are not as acute as mine, that this sense or skill does not exist.'

'Animals', she explained, 'have a far greater sense of smell and hearing than humans, migrating birds have directional instincts which can outclass the most sophisticated apparatus used by airline crews.'

'Some humans', she continued, 'have acute and developed senses and skills which often manifest themselves in sheer genius - this can be most vivid in science, music and art - this is accepted fact! I too have special skills', she went on, 'but I am no witch!'

We all sat mesmerised in a semi-circle around this fascinating storyteller. As the whisky sipping continued and the tongues loosened, the inevitable question begged to be asked. I put it to her. 'How can you demonstrate your special skill, Seer Annie?'

'Well', she said, as if anticipating this moment, 'this is what to do. Go outside the front door of this cottage, and close the door behind you,' she pointed. 'Once there, do something extraordinary, from my position in this seat and in the company of your friends, there can be no hokery-pokery!' she explained.

I rose to the challenge. Satisfied that there were no hidden cameras, mirrors or peeping eyes, I stood outside the front door

JAN
FEB
MAR
APR
MAY
JUNE
JULY
AUG
SEPT
OCT
NOV
DEC

considering my next course of action. I hopped on the spot and turned clockwise three times, repeating this exercise in an anti-clockwise direction. To conclude I scratched my nose, my right knee and left buttock and concluded by pulling a hair out of my head.

'That's it', I thought, 'she'll never get all that.'

I knocked on the door when I was finished.

'Come in sonny', she beckoned, 'and sit yourself down.'

'Well?', I enquired, 'what was I doing out there, Seer Annie?'

'That sonny, is very easy to answer,' she said with an impish grin. 'You were making a bloody fool of yourself!'

Ajax and Mayonnaise

The River Spey or Speyside is to malt whisky what the Gironde is to Bordeaux wines. The Spey, depending on the seasons, meanders or floods through malt whisky country like a life-bringing artery. The river bank is lined with premier cru 'chateaux' such as Glenfarclas, Glenfiddich, Glenlivet, Macallan, Cardhu, Glen Grant, Cragganmore and Aberlour. These are just some of the world famous Speyside malts.

Walking around Kingston at the mouth of the River Spey one hundred years ago, you would have come across a Dutch-style windmill used to power a sawmill. Windmills, tulips, cheese, clogs and Bols genever (grain spirit) are all symbols of a delightful country and people I am very fond of — Holland.

It is not a place to visit if you want to get away from people, in fact it is the third most populated country in the world. On the surface the Dutch are as laid back as the Mediterranean people but they retain a deep-rooted Scots-style thriftiness. As a Scot this makes our Dutch cousins easy to relate to, especially as they also have strong nationalistic tendencies. I was surprised to witness this quite recently when Ajax Amsterdam beat AC Milan in the 1995 European Cup Final. I watched the game in a small pub in Amsterdam. They might just as well have won the World Cup — the city was gripped with football fever for days.

The conquering heroes returned to Amsterdam the following day with their trophy. A Michael Jackson concert could not have attracted so much curiosity. Over 100,000 people crowded into the Museumplein Park awaiting their team's return. As a result of all the excitement, commercialism stepped up a gear. Silvery

JAN
FEB
MAR
APR
MAY
JUNE
JULY
AUG
SEPT
OCT
NOV
DEC

31

European Cup balloons were sold at platinum prices, but what parent could refuse their offspring a souvenir? Also for sale were boldly printed T-shirts with the words WHO THE F**K IS MILANO? Even Schiphol Airport was temporarily closed as the team aircraft circled the city bowing its wings in honour of the winners. Imagine shutting down Heathrow!

Eventually in a roar of mass hysteria, the gladiators appeared on stage, cup in hand. As the amplifiers pumped out Queen's We Are The Champions, you could not help but get caught up in the excitement.

I found myself singing too.

Helicopters circled above as daring youths climbed up trees and lamp posts to secure the best views of their team. A bus shelter creaked and moaned under the weight of swaying hoards of fans. Fireworks banged loudly adding to the general din of rattling bottles and cans kicked by countless feet. The smell of acrid smoke mingled with the oily odours of fried chips and warm mayonnaise. I could not see an Italian face anywhere, I think I too would have stayed at home — some of the lampposts closely resembled hangmen's stocks!

The whole scene reminded me of old cinemascope newsreel depicting the liberation of Paris. It reinforced my belief that deep down European countries are still fiercely nationalistic. The celebrations continued and we headed to a nearby, albeit crowded pub.

Amsterdam should really be avoided by car as the authorities actively discourage drivers. Parking fees are extortionate and should your ticket expire by eight seconds you will be miserably clamped. There are the added obstacles of the Dutch en mass, on bikes, in trams and walking around beside the canals. My advice is leave the car at home!

Like most international cities Amsterdam suffers a sleazy side, with drugs, prostitution and petty crime. You have to be careful as strangers will constantly be brushing shoulders with you and dipping into your pockets. This however, does not spoil the more enjoyable pursuits Holland offers.

Amsterdam is full of character, interesting museums and exhibitions, concerts, arcades, markets, antique shops and the restaurants, pubs and cafés are all wonderfully varied. In the cafés try their spicy breaded meat balls, *bitter ballen* with mustard or the ubiquitous wafer-thin savoury or sweet pancakes. A favourite restaurant of mine is the Haesje Claes on the Spuistraat 275. Its

JAN
FEB
MAR
APR
MAY
JUNE
JULY
AUG
SEPT
OCT
NOV
DEC

namesake Lady Haesje Claes was born in 1520 into a prosperous merchant family. She was the founder and patron of the public orphanage which is now the Amsterdam Historical Museum. The restaurant atmosphere is medieval in its candle-lit, wood-panelled chambers with leaded stained-glass windows, low-beamed ceilings and old tapestries adorning its walls.

The spirit of the mediaeval period lingers throughout the old Dutch chambers where typical 'no-nonsense' dishes are served. Try the herring and smoked eel salad for starters or French-style onion soup, a meal in itself. For main courses the calves' livers in Madeira sauce is delicious. For serious blotting paper I recommend any of the beef, pork or lamb stews. They are accompanied with creamy mashed potatoes, sauerkraut and curly kale served with bacon, sausage and pickles. There is a wide range of fish dishes including sea perch, Dutch shrimps, Dover sole, mussels and herring. You are unlikely to feel hungry after this, however should the sweet tooth prevail, there is an ample choice of desserts.

Just across the street is the restaurant and brasserie, Luden, dramatically different in style but nonetheless charming. It is best described as chic, bright, noisy and busy, so much so you have to book a table early. High ceilings and a huge window at the rear gives the restaurant an airy atmosphere. The cuisine is typically European with Dutch influences. Favoured starters would be the creamy chickory au gratin with Dutch shrimps from Stellendam or the sautéed cod fish fillet with a warm salad of apple, beetroot, potato and raspberry vinaigrette. The lamb's sweetbreads marinated in honey and basil with pasta pesto rosso is divine.

For a main course I loved the grilled angler fish with Noilly Prat sauce, capers, stir-fried spinach and potatoes, but equally delicious is the rack of lamb with black tagliatelle and garlic rosemary sauce. Not having a sweet tooth the warm goat's cheese au gratin with honey and thyme sauce I found to be a marvellous dessert. Both restaurants offered good value eating at approximately 45 guilders each (about £15) per head excluding wine.

A leisurely stroll through the narrow back streets, close to the canal, is like travelling back in time. The narrow facades of the 17th-century dwellings are due to their method of calculating taxes. The narrower the facade the less tax was paid. I feel Scottish frugality surfacing again!

In the countryside every scratch of marketable black earth is utilised, whether it be for flowers, vegetables or under dairy herds. The processed grass from the latter now nourishes the former- nothing is wasted. Coming from the Highlands of Scotland I find the Dutch landscape depressingly flat, but this does have an advantage for cyclists and skaters alike. These items are a birthright for the Dutch, as is their corner kitchen shrine, the coffee maker. The Dutch run on the stuff and perhaps even surpass the French in this respect.

When arriving by ferry Europort Rotterdam is not the best first impression of the Netherlands, but you will soon discover Holland to be a very pleasant location, both on the pocket and culturally. The busy port illustrates how their past and present economy has been derived from trading and distribution. They truck one third of all European road haulage and the port of Rotterdam is one of the world's largest container bases, handling over five million containers per annum.

Dutch shops offer exceptional value for clothes, shoes, tulip bulbs, candles, cheese, wines and beers. Window shopping is available to males as well as females. You can read the menu but dare not take a photo of the local scenery in the red light district, otherwise a screaming pimp or scantily clad lady will appear from nowhere demanding 'artistic fees'!

Hotels and restaurants in the off season, that is in late autumn/early spring, provide good value for tourists. From Scotland Air UK offers a sensibly priced weekend package, with an overnight stay on Saturday which avoids their peak business flights. I recommend Hogmanay because nearly everyone lets off fireworks and exuberance at midnight. You could be mistaken in thinking World War III has broken out. This continues into the wee small hours, even though the temperature outside can be -10c.

JAN
FEB
MAR
APR
MAY
JUNE
JULY
AUG
SEPT
OCT
NOV
DEC

The city the following day is covered in red confetti blossoms as chilling winds scatter the remnants of fireworks across frozen canals. God help the rubbish collectors, it must cost a fortune!

Amsterdam is my second favourite place, after Scotland, to be on Hogmanay. You will certainly be made welcome somewhere by somebody that night. They nearly all speak perfect English, French, German and Dutch.

The Scotch malt whisky connection is the Grant Café De Still sited near the restaurants described earlier at Spuistraat 326. This is a malt whisky lover's haven. A co-operative of 20 dedicated connoisseurs and enthusiasts run this marvellous establishment. You can buy malts by the glass, or if you are local, purchase a whole bottle of your favourite tipple. This will be locked safely away in your own glass-fronted bottle keep. But it has to be consumed within a certain date. You can stumble out of here and step into one of Amsterdam's oldest and most charming hostelries — The Hoppe. A curtain shrouds the entrance to catch chilling winds, but once inside you will be greeted with warmth, humour, joviality and song. Locals savour the Dutch beers and the old genever is highly recommended.

Good hospitality? Look no further than the Scots or Dutch.

Drambusters

Speyside distilleries have never, as yet, been bombed. They are, however, constantly 'targeted' by the local Royal Air Force on low flying training missions. Pagodas and warehouses, I am told, frequently come into the fighter pilot's sights. One silent spring morning in Speyside, I myself, was rudely awakened by screaming jet engines, as Tornados passed overhead at 200 feet, doing 530mph and burning 12 gallons of fuel a minute! Summer visitors get quite startled by their sudden and noisy entrance.

The Speyside/Moray area supports two major military air bases at Kinloss and Lossiemouth which is home to the Second World War 'Dambusters' 617 squadron, once famous with the bouncing bombs, the aircraft now being Tornado fighters.

Kinloss is home to the Nimrod surveillance aircraft used principally by NATO during the cold war to detect Soviet nuclear subs. Nearby lies Findhorn Bay and the picturesque village where sailing boats, fishermen's cottages and quiet pubs set the scene. This coastal village is rumoured to stand above a mediaeval settlement which was engulfed by sand centuries before. Legend has it that one stormy night the local priest played cards and supped whisky with the devil until their dwelling was completely buried by sand!

A good friend, Barrie Chown, a former Fleet Air Arm and RAF Aviator, now trains Tornado crews on the 'simulator' at the base. He survived a mid-air collision, in 1969, by safely ejecting from a Buccaneer before it crashed to earth. The handle which he pulled to release himself is proudly displayed in his restaurant, the 'Abbey Court' in Elgin, which he runs with his wife Helen. This

JAN
FEB
MAR
APR
MAY
JUNE
JULY
AUG
SEPT
OCT
NOV
DEC

splendid bistro stocks a fine range of wines, malts and the house ale is Belhaven. They make everyone welcome, Barrie himself flits from table to table resembling the Basil Fawlty character. Over the years I have got to know him very well, and have thoroughly enjoyed hearing his many stories from the flying world. Although they are too many to tell, I have chosen three I believe to be classics.

Barrie's Stories
1. FOXTROT DELTA
Despite being assured that aviators are not superstitious, they do have some pretty quirky 'lucky charms', often manifesting themselves in the form of squadron mascots. Remember Guy Gibson's black lab Nigger who became legendary during the Dambusters' bombing sorties? It was during one of these raids that the dog was run down in camp and tragically his master didn't return. Today Nigger's remains are buried under the squadron's ceremonial flagpole and rumour has it that they are to be exhumed when the squadron moves to a new camp. Superstitious, or what?

Another squadron that had a mascot was the No 12(B) flying Vulcan bombers. Prior to Polaris and Trident nuclear submarines, the Vulcan bomber served as a valuable and crucial deterrent mechanism. This beautiful delta-winged aircraft could deliver its terrible cargo of mass destruction from the heavenly heights of 35,000 feet. It was also used in low-level bombing runs during the Falklands War.

In the sixties and early seventies these aircraft were regular visitors to the Morayshire airbases. One squadron commander had taken the mascot business to the extreme, and for ceremonial purposes adopted a real dog fox. The mascot was kitted out with a leather lead, studded collar and ceremonial coat. The most junior pilot (JP) had the onerous job of looking after Mr Fox, and became known as 'Officer in Charge of Fox'. One duty involved getting up at the crack of dawn to exercise the animal across the airfield.

It was during one of these early mornings drills that disaster struck. Basil fox must have got wind of an awaiting Samantha on the air base

perimeter. He slipped his lead, and like a bullet, sped towards his lusty companion. His journey and heightened passion were short-lived. On the main runway a 60-ton Vulcan bomber was landing at 160mph. Basil was certainly in the wrong place at the wrong time. The distraught JP searched and searched for his remains, only to discover his hairy-outline, etched onto the runway tarmac. He carefully unrolled the mat-like coat and placed it under his arm. 'Basil's been struck by some bad luck, Boss', he explained to the squadron commander.

The Vulcans are no more, but No 12(B) Squadron can still be seen flying Tornado fighter aircraft over Lossiemouth. The fox is still their mascot, but there are no more Basils — BOOM BOOM!

JAN
FEB
MAR
APR
MAY
JUNE
JULY
AUG
SEPT
OCT
NOV
DEC

2. OVER THE SKY TO SEA

During his flying career Barrie was often stationed overseas. It was while in Laarbruch, Germany, during the seventies, that this particularly embarrassing incident took place. One of his tasks was to help organise the summer ball, a goodwill public relations exercise. This was a traditional annual event, where the boat, sorry aircraft, would be pushed out. His task was to procure such delicacies as fresh seafood and malt whisky.

As it happened, Barrie knew of a forthcoming training exercise, to be held in an area rich in such delicacies, and only two days before the ball. The place was Lossiemouth, Morayshire. The Buccaneer aircraft could stop overnight there and return the next morning to Laarbruch. Barrie also knew that the aircraft were not armed and therefore there was room for tastier cargoes in the bomb bays. Mafia-style arrangements were conducted with Mr 'John The Fish' of Lossiemouth as boxes of fresh lobster, crab, prawns, shrimps and smoked Speyside salmon were stowed discreetly by co-conspirators in the bomb bays alongside a cache of fine malt whisky.

In the morning the unsuspecting pilots took the aircraft out to sea; the skies clear, perfect conditions for training. The formation leader commenced the sortie with a full simulated attack on imaginary shipping. All the aircraft took part. The attack checklist commenced. The navigator who was in on the act, but was suffering from a slight lapse in memory called out, 'Weapons selector! Attack selector . . . station selector . . . accept bar safety catch . . . trigger firing catch . . . bomb doors open — CHRIST, THE FISH!'

On arriving at Laarbruch hours later, and checking the bomb bays, the only remains of their gourmet extravaganza was one dismembered lobster claw and two miserable prawns. That year the summer ball menu consisted of a selection of bratwurst on

JAN
FEB
MAR
APR
MAY
JUNE
JULY
AUG
SEPT
OCT
NOV
DEC

sticks and Frankfurters with chips, served by a very red-faced Buccaneer crew!

3. THE TYPISSED

It was while stationed in Aalborg, Denmark, that Barrie nearly lost more than his flying suit. He had just completed a hairy low-level night flying sortie, and was totally hyped up on landing. It was 22.00 hours and he relaxed over a pint of beer in the officers' mess. Knowing that he was now on three days' leave the pints were downed at an increasingly faster rate. He then noticed some Danish colleagues in the bar and a conversation ensued. They were moving on to a party off-base and cordially invited Barrie along. On being invited to dinners or parties by overseas personnel, it was customary to sign out the 'typewriter' held in the mess bar. This was nothing less than a 'mobile bar' which looked deceptively innocent hidden in its typewriter-style carrying case. Inside, however, could be found Speyside malt whisky and four crystal glasses. So, with 'typewriter' in hand and still wearing his flying suit, he jauntily set off for the party with his Danish colleagues.

On arriving at the private house he was puzzled by the fact that a code seemed to be used to ring the doorbell. He quickly forgot any doubts when a beautiful young blonde girl opened the door. She was starkers. Barrie grinned and offered the typewriter. Another nude appeared, this time male, and warmly greeted the visitors.

Slowly but surely, through the drunken haze, as men danced with men, women with women, Barrie realised the nature of the gathering. As males fondled the zips on his flying suit he decided it was time for a sharp exit. He grabbed the typewriter only to find the front door locked so he made a hasty retreat to the kitchen. A huge pivot-style window met him there, and deciding it was his

JAN
FEB
MAR
APR
MAY
JUNE
JULY
AUG
SEPT
OCT
NOV
DEC

only means of escape, he jumped out of the window, typewriter in hand. Unbeknown to him, the rear of the house was built on a hill with a 20ft drop to the garden! Landing on top of a berberis bush, without a parachute, only his pride was injured — even the typewriter and its precious contents survived intact!

Some locals do not appreciate air personnel, but without their presence, there would not be the spending power and wealth so evident in the towns. There would not be, for sure, so many good pubs and restaurants (three Indian restaurants alone!), cinemas, night clubs, not to mention the more cosmopolitan atmosphere due to people well travelled. Being a local, I can say with confidence, that the wide range of real ales and malt whiskies offered 'in town' is a result of this.

Lastly, for those intrepid aviators with Glenfarclas Distillery in your sights, please, please, never ever, press that red button!

Home from Holmes

My first trip through the Channel Tunnel was the 4 February 1995. I can recall this date easily as I requested a stamp in my passport as a souvenir. I took the Eurostar passenger train from Gare du Nord, Paris direct to Waterloo, London within three and half hours. It is a much easier journey than flying from Paris to London which requires connecting tubes and buses into the city centre. Eurostar will surely be a success, especially if we improve the rail system at our end.

Every half hour, Le Shuttle leaves Dover for Calais carrying vehicles and passengers quickly and smoothly to their destination. You simply drive up to the terminal, buy a ticket and if all goes well you are on board in 20 minutes, and on your way in ten. The space-age engine has a streamlined body, strongly resembling a plane. Behind the engine are the long tubes of carriages which are sectioned off into compartments when all the cars have boarded. You remain in the car throughout the 35-minute journey. Passengers are instructed to leave a car window open to reduce the force of the air pressure in the carriage. It is a strange sensation travelling hundreds of feet under the channel for the first time.

One drizzly Sunday morning in July, I arrived in Dover ready to drive on board but I was astonished to see how dirty and grimy Le Shuttle had become. There before me stood a grubby train spattered with grease and grime. What a shame, all it needed was a damned good clean. The impression of neglect would not inspire confidence in a wary traveller.

My trip this month was to take me through France and Luxembourg ending the week in Switzerland. Despite the strong

JAN
FEB
MAR
APR
MAY
JUNE
JULY
AUG
SEPT
OCT
NOV
DEC

Swiss franc (or rather the weaker European currencies), it is a good market for malt whisky. Switzerland is not cheap at the best of times — a standard bottle of ten-year-old malt whisky will set you back £43. The duty element is even higher than the UK and that takes some beating! To get this into perspective the same standard bottle of malt around the other major European markets retails from anything from 20-40 per cent cheaper than in the UK. In Italy, for example, a bottle will cost you £12 and in Germany £15. The UK is quite different at well over £20 a bottle.

It is a pleasure to observe your product being actively purchased by consumers in foreign countries. Sometimes at home you can wait a long time to observe a sale. A basic and standard practice by sales people is to run a finger over the top of the bottles. Dust is a good indication of the rate of sale. No, I am not being rude about their housekeeping — tops of bottles are easily forgotten and indeed some stores actively encourage a little dust to settle on old malts and wines for authenticity! The point I am making is that dust is less obvious in countries that sensibly tax whisky. Unless prices for such commodities are in line with the rest of Europe, what chance is there for a single European currency?

My appointments concluded in Zurich on Friday afternoon and I was free to explore the countryside. I decided to make my way up to the mountains and find an inexpensive little chalet hotel to rest over for the weekend. Also I was eager to dump the car having driven over 2,000 miles that week. My journey took me in the direction of Interlaken, and on nearing the town I noticed a signpost for Meiringen. Bells rang in my head. This must be the place famous for none other than Mr Sherlock Holmes, the detective character created by the Scot, Sir Arthur Conan Doyle. Holmes was the first to apply pure logic to solving mysterious crimes, and his emulators are now numbered in thousands.

Meiringen is famous, of course, for the Reichenbach Falls where the character met his demise at the hands of his arch-enemy Moriarty. It is now home to the Sherlock Holmes Museum, in a delightful little church with a basement exhibition depicting that famous Victorian salon, where enigmas would be unlocked. Doubtless our Mr Holmes would have indulged in a fine malt whisky to assist in these matters, a decanter or two of which were on the mahogany dresser!

I was drawn to the Reichenbach Falls like a magnet. Disappointment prevailed at the trolley car station, it was closed due to maintenance work. I persevered and enquired of a young lady who was passing.

'You can drive up part of the way', she explained, 'then its another fifteen minutes walk from the Schwendi Hotel'. I'll go for this, I thought! Then I realised the only route was a sheer mountain track. Wincing at the thought of brake failure I imagined the headlines in newspapers . . . *Whisky Rep Meets His Doom At Reichenbach Falls.* I continued upwards nonetheless. Reaching the hotel an elderly matron greeted me with more than a hint of distrust in her eyes. Yes, she obviously

JAN
FEB
MAR
APR
MAY
JUNE
JULY
AUG
SEPT
OCT
NOV
DEC

47

thought I was mad climbing this mountain but she kindly pointed me in the right direction towards the falls. I promised to return for a refreshment soon, hoping this indeed would be the case as I was worried I might end up following in Sherlock's footsteps.

In the distance could be heard the thundering sound of water crashing onto the rocks below. The path was lightly worn and I assumed that few people had come this way before. It was exciting stuff embarking on the unknown, goose pimples made me shiver and my heart raced. I scrambled uphill, then turned a corner and climbed over a primitive gate, clambered over shingle and slate, with the footing slippery and crumbling. At last, there cascading from a sheer rock overhang, plummeting downwards into the abyss below, were the stunning Reichenbach Falls. The natural scale was intimidating, but a fine spray refreshed my brow.

This was a strange haunting place, full of danger and drama. Mr Holmes could not have survived such a drop!

I later discovered that Moriarty lived near Piccadilly in Half Moon Street which was coincidentally the home of The Scotch Whisky Association, until recently. Last year they moved to the more aptly named 14 Cork Street!

Twelve Trestle Virgins

This is a tale about the 'glorious' 12th of August, the start of the shooting season. It was a splendidly hot opening day on the grouse moors of Scotland. I was sitting in the Fiddichside Inn in Craigellachie, a delightful Speyside village. Its pronunciation, CRAIG-ELL-ACHIE has confounded overseas and English visitors alike and it is often shortened to 'The Craig'. The coolness of the tiny pub and the dark, cold beer was refreshing as I sat chatting with the regulars. They were mainly country folk, some famous ghillies and gamekeepers accompanied by their black Labrador gun dogs that in winter snooze idly in front of the generous log fire.

The theme of the conversation was much to do with hunting, shooting and fishing. It came to light in the course of the banter that there exists an 'exclusive club' of hunters who have passed the formidable test of the McNabe. To achieve this distinguished feat, the hunter has 24 hours, to catch a fresh run Spey salmon, stalk and despatch a red deer stag, and down a driven grouse. A formidable task indeed!

Not to be outclassed, a young ghillie piped up, 'Naw, naw . . . that's old hat' he explained. 'The Royal McNabe is the real test'.

'Royal McNabe, Royal McNabe?' demanded a gruff voice. 'Yes, and not only do you have to shoot a deer, a grouse and catch a salmon you must also make love to a virgin from Inverness!' A silence ensued. Then one thoughtful wee voice exclaimed, 'Well, that's bloody impossible, there ain't any virgins left in Inverness!'

Dorothy Brandie and her husband Joe have run the Fiddichside Inn since 1946. Dorothy was born in nearby Dufftown, in the

JAN
FEB
MAR
APR
MAY
JUNE
JULY
AUG
SEPT
OCT
NOV
DEC

49

Commercial Hotel to be exact. I mention this as the owners are now a George and Edna Buchan. They offer the best value for money nosh I have ever tasted. The meat roll is outstanding and the brisket and meallie pudding with veg is memorable. George Buchan deserves this accolade. Hot, wholesome winter fuel at its best AND with change from a fiver. Back to the Fiddichside.

Authentic Victorian mirrors grace the walls of what must be Scotland's smallest bar — ten

people are a crowd here. The original oak bar top sports a patina which represents countless years of service, the comforting sound of a clock ticking can be heard during breaks in the chatter. The sign above the bar proclaims it as 'headquarters for fishermen, husbands and other liars'.

During the summer months fresh sandwiches are the favoured pub grub here. If lucky, as I was, you may be offered poached salmon, which is steamed in wine vinegar, not stolen! Dorothy refused to take any money from me as she said she had too much fish left and it would not last in the heat. It was delicious, sea-run with that tangy, salty-water taste, mingled with earthy-mushroomy flavours absorbed from the peaty river.

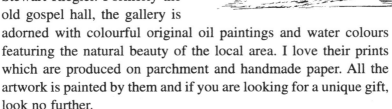

Strolling into the village you will come across the Green Gallery, where a warm welcome awaits from Maggie and Stewart Riegler. Formerly the old gospel hall, the gallery is adorned with colourful original oil paintings and water colours featuring the natural beauty of the local area. I love their prints which are produced on parchment and handmade paper. All the artwork is painted by them and if you are looking for a unique gift, look no further.

Of all the hotels I have stayed in at home and abroad, the Craigellachie takes some beating. It is located in the centre of the village overlooking the River Spey, and you could not envisage a more idyllic setting. The architectural style is elegant, typical of a grand Victorian highland home. You can relax here and unwind with the help of the friendly yet unobtrusive staff.

The cocktail bar stocks over 250 malt whiskies, no one as yet has sampled them all! The most expensive dram, a Black Bowmore 1964 vintage will set you back £23. The hotel itself has a strong whisky connection. The architect Charles C Doig who

JAN
FEB
MAR
APR
MAY
JUNE
JULY
AUG
SEPT
OCT
NOV
DEC

designed it in 1893 was also famous for distillery commissions. Indeed he instigated the oriental-style 'pagodas' (malting chimneys), a feature of many Speyside distilleries.

The cuisine here makes full use of the prime local produce as the area is abundant in game, beef and seafood. Internationally acclaimed chefs work here, however they do not come cheap, so their 'Highland Banquet' dinner of six courses will set you back nearly £40. But for that special occasion it is definitely worth it. The Rib Room menu fits different pockets and boasts some mouth-watering delights: guinea fowl breast with celery purée, bacon and pesto or try the casserole of monkfish with broad beans, shallots and tomato butter sauce and venison loin with red cabbage, woodland mushrooms and port sauce. There are so many main courses to choose from, all at about £13. The desserts can be as light or heavy as you wish. Afterwards, comfy sofas will engulf and embalm you in front of the warming open fires, an aperitif of smooth and aged malt and then bed beckons . . .

The Highland retreat would not be complete without the resident ghost. Many guests, in room number 224, have reported a presence, albeit a pleasant one. Perhaps it could even be the spirit of Thomas Telford, the famous 19th century Scots road and bridge builder. Looking out from the hotel bedroom you can see a fine example of his work. The old 'Craig Bridge', built in 1814, spans the river in a beautiful steel arch, with two stone turrets on either side.

Taking the high road out of the Craig towards Dufftown, you will discover the Speyside Cooperage, or rather it will discover you! Mountains of barrels, old and new, rise up from behind their visitor centre. Many moons ago, around mid-summer, travelling tinkers gathered round the peripheries of distilleries and cooperages alike, where barrels were stored. These men were after the 'billings' which are the very last drops of whisky left in an emptied cask. Today housekeeping is much stricter.

Let me try to explain more about barrel making. 'Cask' is the name given to describe all whisky barrels but they are not actually called barrels, as a 'barrel' is a size of cask. Lost yet? Well, a barrel holds 180 litres, a hogshead ('hoggie') 250 litres, and a sherry 'butt', 500 litres. The smallest cask used by smugglers, the 'anker', contained 20 Scots pints (about 20 litres).

The bigger casks were often used in mediaeval times as a type of 'torture stocks' for drunkards, where holes were cut out for arms and legs and the cask hinged through the centre to allow access.

All casks are made from oak which allows maturing whisky to breath and be massaged by the local microclimate. After many long years spent maturing in cool dark cellars, the casks are removed for bottling. Empty casks usually return to the parent distillery or cooperage for repair, to be used again. After the cask is emptied the bungs (corks) are replaced.

A recently emptied cask will start to dry out very quickly. This is accelerated in the summer heat, and most good warehousemen will hose down casks on a hot day to prevent the wood drying out. But you always get a certain amount of shrinkage. This effect reminds me of wringing a sponge, squeezing the last drops of whisky out of the pores of the wood. These last drops are known affectionately as 'billings', and although woody tasting, like a Spanish Rioja wine, it is, I am told, perfectly good whisky! Hence the strong interest from the tinkers. A 'good cask' is said to produce a 'saucepan' of whisky. The 'bung' is first removed and then the cask is rolled over, bung down, over a strong metal saucepan, and voilà! The bungs are replaced, to give an impression that the cask has never been tampered with.

To learn more on casks and coopering in general, the Speyside Cooperage is highly recommended as the finest working example. The craftsmen are a pleasure to observe as the muscle-bound coopers waltz with their rounded partners. A flaming torch is used to scorch the insides of casks and the overall effect reminds me of the church scene from Burns' Tam O' Shanter.

JAN
FEB
MAR
APR
MAY
JUNE
JULY
AUG
SEPT
OCT
NOV
DEC

The Speyside Way (a country walk of 42 miles through Speyside) intersects Craigellachie on its way southwards to Tomintoul or westwards to Dufftown. If you join it at Craigellachie and travel onwards to Ballindalloch-Tomintoul you will start to cross moorland and hill ground and in places travel along 16th-century cart and drove roads. It is not too difficult to imagine this landscape hiding illicit stills and bothies with smugglers on the lookout for excisemen!

My last stop was the Tomintoul Brewery, the highest brewery in Scotland at 1164 feet above sea level. It was founded by David Sole (the former Scotland 1990 'Grand Slam' rugby skipper) around Christmas 1993. This tiny micro-brewery produces traditional real ales of outstanding quality which is little wonder as the mountain water used feeds the River Spey. The brewery is based in a converted 18th-century mill and its magical burn is known as the Conglass Water. They use malted barley, hops and pure glen water to produce authentic highland ales which are full-bodied, malty with plenty of hops. As yet the brewery is too small to facilitate casual visitors, but you can sample the scrumptious end-product in the many and varied hostelries in the surrounding neighbourhood.

One example 'Tomintoul Stag', a dark delicious malty bitter is also available in bottles. My favourite however, is Lairds Ale (ABV 3.8%) a traditional Scottish 70/- which is malty with a light hop balance. For the real bravehearts, try the 'Highland Hammer' (ABV 7.3%), full-flavoured strong ale.

I think I'm beginning to feel the effect of the high altitude already!

Ground Mice, Fungi and the Appliance of Science

This was the month I was honoured by an invitation from Dr Antony Zanussi to the Villa Frattina in Northern Italy. He was the first high-powered industrialist I had ever met. He was not simply a 'businessman', but created the Zanussi company renowned for its slogan 'The Appliance of Science'. Strike action in the eighties seriously disrupted production in his many factories. The Italian government was so concerned with the dire consequences of reduced exports upsetting the balance of payments, that they eventually bought out and 'nationalised' Zanussi. This made Mr Zanussi a very rich man indeed.

On leaving the 'white goods' business he bought the Villa Frattina with its vast cellars of fine wines. He marketed these extremely well and included malt whisky and other fine spirits in his portfolio. He was a mysterious man as he rarely left the sanctuary of the well-guarded chateau-style house situated in the original grounds.

Our invitation was to a celebration dinner party to mark the end of the grape-picking season. The venue was a large warehouse, draped in white silk. I could not have imagined that I was about to savour one of the finest meals I have ever eaten. Without going into gourmet-style jargon, it will suffice to say that the food was rustic, simple and varied. The nine course menu consisted of nearly six hours of gobsmacking flavours, continually washed down with luscious light wines. Each course was a surprise, and just sufficient in quantity not to fill you up

JAN
FEB
MAR
APR
MAY
JUNE
JULY
AUG
SEPT
OCT
NOV
DEC

55

completely, and thus keep your appetite fresh. It was the flavours and tastes that were paramount, not the amount of food. That said, we were completely satisfied by the end of the night.

Incredibly, we were seated next to the great man himself who carried himself like a great Roman emperor. I imagined his ancestors, giving the thumbs down signal to gladiators battling in the arena. This evening it was thumbs up all round as it was my first serious introduction to the delights of the mushroom species. Morels, ceps and chanterelles featured in many dishes, adding rich aromatic flavours, perfectly complemented by our host's choice of wine. The evening concluded with a superb performance by one of Italy's famous magicians Silvan. This was not the usual pulling rabbits out of hats, instead we witnessed the sawing in half of beautiful hostesses and not a drop of blood lost. This was truly a wonderful and mystical experience.

Mr Zanussi eventually sold the villa and I have found it difficult to find out anything more about him. The Sicilian Averna family now own the property and market the wines. They have good distribution links throughout Italy, and also market Glenfarclas malt whisky as well as other spirits. The Italian malt whisky market is excellent and has become one of the strongest in Europe. Seagram's brand Glen Grant 5 year old dominates the Italian market. Their share is in excess of 80 per cent and a mind-blowing half a million twelve-bottle cases are sold per annum. This success must be credited to the marketing skills of Armando Giovinetti. The product itself is light and easy on the palate and this fits the bill for long lazy Mediterranean evenings.

People ask, who, if anyone, can steal this business. One lady springs to mind, Cristina Calasso our brand manager with Averna in Milan. She is an energetic and enthusiastic marketing executive. On the conclusion of a recent sales meeting in Milan she invited me for lunch at the Ristorante Tre Pini. On entering the restaurant I was overwhelmed by the delicious aromas of freshly cut basil and oregano, garlic, olive oil and parmesan cheese. My stomach rumbled loudly in response to these delights. The menu was in Italian but Cristina translated for me in excellent English as my Italian is nearly non-existent. However, the language barrier still caused a humorous misunderstanding. She smiled sweetly as she read an entry for a main course. 'Oh good', she remarked, 'a typical country dish is offered, which reminds me of my childhood in Sicily.' Mushrooms, I thought, but no. I got caught up in her excitement and enquired if I could choose this dish too.

'Certainly', she exclaimed, 'but do you like ground mice?' A silence followed.

'Ground mice', I questioned.

'Yes, ground mice', she replied. 'You probably get this in Scotland too, but we grind ours down into a mash, a typical country dish'.

At this point Tommy Dewar's book *A Ramble round the Globe* came to mind. In this he described a dining experience in Hong Kong around the turn of the century. 'We did not', he explains, 'try that peculiarly Chinese epicurean dish Blind Mice, and I don't think I should care to do so either. 'They call this "Milhi" which really means "mice"; they are placed alive on a small tray before each guest, who, taking them one by one by the tail, dips them in honey, then swallows them! It is said that when the Emperor's wedding was celebrated a few years ago, 50,000 of these young mice were consumed at the banquet.'

'Are they dead before you grind them', I enquired?

'Dead? As dead as any vegetable can be', she explained.

'Vegetable?'

'Yes, vegetable', she said looking puzzled. 'They grow on cobs in fields.'

'Oh . . . maize', I said with a sigh of relief. 'Yes, ground mice', she reiterated.

Or as we know it, polenta!

JAN
FEB
MAR
APR
MAY
JUNE
JULY
AUG
SEPT
OCT
NOV
DEC

What strikes me most about Italians is their insatiable appetite for good fashion and gastronomy and they are world leaders in both. For what it's worth, I believe their cuisine to be the finest in the world. It fashions other European dishes. Italian restaurants are found throughout the world and renowned for the excellent culinary skills. Scotland boasts its fair share thanks to the many Italian families who emigrated many years ago to make their fortunes here. They introduced many new dishes which rapidly became popular.

One such person, Mario Cabrelli arrived in Tayport, Fife from Pontremolli in Tuscany in October 1937. At 12 years of age, with no knowledge of spoken English, he came to join his father who ran a café there. He came from an area in the mountains, rich in culinary delights with an appreciation of good food and drink. He instinctively sensed how things should look and taste. Even as late as the sixties there was only one thing worse than traditional English meat-and-two-veg, and that was what passed for Scottish cuisine. These must have been hard times for such a family.

As a young boy growing up in Tuscany, Mario discovered his grandmother's knowledge of mushrooms. He would spend days on end seeking them out. These were then eaten raw with olive oil, peppers and finely chopped garlic or dried in the sun for two days and then stored in muslin bags. These were used throughout the winter by his grandmother who added them to sauces and stew. This is a hobby he has indulged in ever since.

In the area of Umbria the wild fungi and truffle are now big business. There is even a 'classification' as with the DOC system for wine on the quality of fungi, the regions of Toscana and Emilia being particularly famous for these delicacies.

I first came to know Mario during my schooldays when he ran the famous Lido Café in Elgin. He was well liked and commanded much respect and he was always sympathetic during exam times.

His coffee was fantastic, years before cappuccino or espresso reached the area. The café still exists, still with its beautiful art deco panelling inside.

For a short time after his retirement he worked as a tourist guide at Glenfarclas Distillery. There he developed a good nose for whisky, favouring the Glenfarclas 30 year-old. He was invaluable in dealing with Italian visitors during the summer months and helped enormously with trade visitors. It was during this time I learned of his 'passion' for mushrooms, and his skills in gathering them. His knowledge is enormous and Mario professes that he can detect the aromatic presence of ceps on entering a wooded glade. I can easily believe him. Speyside ceps have been in demand, for that special occasion, in Antonio Carluccio's famous Neal Street restaurant in London. This is a mecca for mushroom lovers where the menu consists almost entirely of fungi or fungi-related dishes.

It is a little known fact that the Speyside area, which provides the wonderful water and maturing conditions for malt whisky, also creates the ideal environment for wild

JAN
FEB
MAR
APR
MAY
JUNE
JULY
AUG
SEPT
OCT
NOV
DEC

mushrooms — dampness and warmth during the summer months.

Many wild mushrooms appear around the distillery in the autumn. One day there is nothing, then suddenly a proliferation of fungi. This besides, and common to all distilleries, we have one visitor all year round. As whisky matures in oak barrels, a small amount of evaporation takes place. The vapours permeate the warehouse walls causing blackening — an effect evident in French wine cellars as well. The discoloration is caused by a minute fungus or spore which thrives on alcohol vapours. They are, however, too small to be harvested. What a pity!

Tight Whalers and Philibegs

The invitation read:

Alcoholic Beverage Mission to Toronto, Montreal and Halifax
19-30 October 1996.

Only the Department of Trade and Industry could have come up with such a tantalising offer. The cocktail of participants would include some of the finest producers of real ales, malt whiskies and gins offered from the UK. It was a recipe for success, the crew as varied as the products they represented. I looked forward to this trip as I recalled an earlier Scottish Tourist Board roadshow that took place in the USA many years before.

Observing group behaviour is fascinating especially when sales personnel are gathered together. At a very early stage there seems to be a 'settling ground' where personalities and characters feel inclined to stamp out a pecking order just like rutting deer. Once these formalities are established, all is well and the bag of game gelled together.

Stamina has to be high on such excursions because of a demanding itinerary. Throughout our visit we would be invited to present our products to the various Liquor Control boards of these regions, visit retail outlets, meet sales agents, local licensees and trade journalists. Our charming Canadian hosts made us feel very welcome and I found this trip enormously rewarding, albeit our products are well represented in those markets already. For most

JAN
FEB
MAR
APR
MAY
JUNE
JULY
AUG
SEPT
OCT
NOV
DEC

61

of the mission participants, this was uncharted territory. My function was more on reinforcing commitments, brand building and offering tastings.

One such evening was particularly memorable. Ian Hanna, our agent in Toronto, had organised a whisky tasting to the north of the city. It was held in the immaculate Hobby Horse pub, an 18th-century wooden-built townhouse. The basement pub stocks a fine range of malt whiskies and real ales and was an excellent location for a tasting. The ambience was created with crackling log fires, low-beamed ceilings, candlelight and intimate tables — a perfect atmosphere.

Volumes have been written on wine and whisky tasting and many writers fall into the all too familiar trap of overpowering the reader with technical detail, and elitist, pretentious prattle. For many years I have conducted countless whisky tastings with all sorts of people at home and abroad. This is a role often described as 'brand ambassadorship'. This experience has prompted me to compile a short synopsis on conducting a simple malt whisky tasting and this can be found at the rear of the book.

Tastings can be exhilarating and fun at best, or a bore and a drudge at worst (avoid the latter like the plague). Dark and wintry evenings are best, I find, when people are looking for something different to do, to learn a bit, and have a good supper afterwards. I thoroughly recommend this as a great evening out.

Our tasting in the Hobby Horse was one of the exhilarating kind. A piper had been organised and the tasters were also in fine tune as everyone joined in with the banter. This presentation was a 'double act', half Scottish and half Canadian, and worked well. On conclusion, I was overwhelmed by the local goodwill and departed with a huge hamper stuffed with maple syrup, jams and comb honey. I later learned from Ian that the Hobby Horse in former times had been a brothel! My illusions were shattered!

The alcoholic mission ended in the charming port of Halifax, Nova Scotia. Many Scots emigrated here during the Highland Clearances and there is still a distinctive Celtic air about the place. Bruce Williams from the Heather Ale Brewery went down a treat here. For the entire mission he wore an early version of the kilt, the philibeg, used by Highland clansmen in the 17th century. This was simply a piece of heavy, oily woollen yarn, six metres by two and dyed using only natural ingredients, such as heather. For daytime use it was spread on the ground over a waist belt and then pleated. The owner would then lie down on it pulling one end over the shoulder and down in front of his body, finally securing it with the belt. At night he simply slept in it.

Our last day in Halifax was a Sunday and a day off. Some bright spark had organised a seafaring trip to observe whales. Departing at midday on a largish fishing boat we berthed five hours later. Joe the skipper, a Para Handy character, reflected the mood of the entourage — a little dour but great company. Stories were exchanged in the galley as the boat bucked through the freezing squalls.

The skipper was distraught, here he was on board with purveyors of some of the finest beverages on offer from the UK, and none of them had remembered to bring the 'kerry oot'. Well, well, well. This grave situation reminded me of a Macallan

JAN
FEB
MAR
APR
MAY
JUNE
JULY
AUG
SEPT
OCT
NOV
DEC

advertisement a few years ago. A ghillie having suffered a disastrous morning's fishing with two clients, asked for a wee dram.

'Nae fish . . . nae Macallan', came the cold reply. The day then passed by quite fruitlessly, and on departing the ghillie gruffly cursed his patrons, 'Nae Macallan . . . nae fish!'

I wondered if Joe, our skip, was of the same school for there were 'nae whales' seen that day!

The last evening in Halifax, developed into an impromptu ceilidh and quickly warmed our sea-numbed bones. But first of all food beckoned and we were all ravenous after our excursion. Experienced sailors know a port's best hostelries are found along the historic properties, one block back from the waterfront. That's where we found the unique O'Carroll's Irish restaurant and pub. Donegal-born Jim O'Carroll is the heart of the place, always greeting new arrivals, spinning yarns, ensuring everyone has a good time. The uncomplicated restaurant menu has various tantalising appetisers, main courses and desserts. The fillet of halibut en papillote on a julienne of sweet peppers enhanced with citrus butter was outstanding. The gaiety of the adjoining bar spilled into the dining room, adding to the boisterous atmosphere. Lyrical Irish melodies and spirited sea shanties enhanced our enjoyment, allowing us to forget that in the morning we would all be returning home by plane.

I wonder what Tommy Dewar would have thought of modern air travel? His sales trips were cruises across the oceans on luxury 'Empress' steam liners that took months, not weeks to complete. Nowadays, only bottled Scotch is carried by sea as the salesmen soar overhead.

Without doubt the aircraft is the most common form of transport used for sales trips abroad. The 747, in particular, has shrunk the world and allowed for far greater access to foreign markets. Indeed, *The Economist* magazine's list of modern-day wonders of the world included the Boeing 747. But although statistics prove it is safer to travel by air than road, there is still that nagging feeling of helplessness, should something go

JAN
FEB
MAR
APR
MAY
JUNE
JULY
AUG
SEPT
OCT
NOV
DEC

dreadfully wrong. There can be few modern inventions which have inspired such a perverse mix of pleasure and terror and many passengers express a silent prayer on take-off, myself included.

Our overnight flight from Toronto was however pleasant and jovial, a few drams were enjoyed and on arrival at Heathrow the sales trip came to an abrupt end. Everyone went their separate ways, mission accomplished.

Something in the Air

In the course of making international sales and the like, you meet some very beautiful and intelligent women. I met Alexandra at the World Travel Market at Earl's Court, London, in November 1992. I described our meeting in my first book *A Nip Around the World*.

'She stood there tall and graceful. No jewellery at all. Just a tiny black dress and matching velvet shoes. I caught her eyes first, dark and smouldering. Perfect eyebrows, small nose and pouting mouth in rich ruby red. Tiny curls clustered around her temples. The curves of her bosom were slightly pronounced and she had a tiny waist with legs that never seemed to end. I looked away, turned and looked back. She performed exactly the same exercise and we caught each other's glance and our mutual embarrassment. This time however her lips turned upwards into the most gorgeous smile. The slight dimples in her cheeks deepened and I am sure I detected the slightest blush. Our eyes held for what seemed like eternity. Oh! I simply must greet this lady, I thought.'

At this point Tommy Dewar's personal tales of travel and selling whisky abroad came to mind again. He was visiting New Zealand in the 1890's and came upon the 'landlord's niece' at the Tarawera Hotel. 'Never before had I thought of the loneliness of a bachelor's life; never before had I thought of the happiness of a married life; never before had I felt my heart turning to wax, and wax of the softest nature.'

Sandra, as I call her, worked in Burgundy at the time and I visited her the following May. She met me at Charles de Gaulle airport, Paris. We were both nervous at first, stopping

JAN
FEB
MAR
APR
MAY
JUNE
JULY
AUG
SEPT
OCT
NOV
DEC

intermittently on the journey south to savour a cigarette. The haunting music of Vangelis' *1492* which she played heightened the electric atmosphere. A strange, wonderfully relaxed mood developed, not sexual to begin with, but that of just talking, laughing and touching hands. It was comfortable and warming. We had no idea that we were embarking on a much longer and tortuous journey.

Three hours later we arrived in Beaune and knowing of my interest in wines and spirits, Sandra had arranged a visit to one of Burgundy's famous vineyards at the Chateau Louis la Tour. We were greeted warmly by her friends Mark and Coreen at the bureaux office in town. Before our trip we relaxed for a short while over a glass of chilled chardonnay. Mark informed us that the vineyard was only a short drive away and we were to follow his car. He assured us this would be easy because his car had a Belgian number plate.

We left the office with a feeling of well-being and climbed into Sandra's car. The Belgian car was a little ahead of us down the street, and as it pulled out we began to follow. Keeping a respectful distance we soon emerged into the green, gently undulating countryside. I was in a dream-like state bathed in the soft warm light, Sandra fell mysteriously quiet, as there was no need to talk.

My curiosity was aroused by the number of small cemeteries we passed en route. These were positioned in the centre of the vineyards. Sandra explained it was a long-standing tradition to bury wine makers and vineyard workers alongside the vines they had tended. I remarked to Sandra, that this was a fitting end, their bones returning to the soil, nourishing it even!

She laughed and we both lost track of time as we continued to follow the other car. Some time passed and we started to get agitated, remembering Mark's description of the 'nearby' vineyard. As if sensing this, the car in front pulled in for some petrol. We pulled over too, and jumped out to appeal to Mark for an end to this journey. There in front of us stood two complete strangers, amazed by our interest in them. We had followed the

wrong car! Sandra resolved the situation with a brief phone call, and without much fuss we soon met up with our friends again. It was now too late to visit the chateau, however Mark had booked a remote country restaurant for dinner. Later that evening we all laughed heartily about our mistake.

The enchanting restaurant was located deep in a forest. I remember a glowing log fire that smouldered against whitewashed walls. It was very quiet and dimly lit although I kept catching glints from Sandra's dark eyes. We tried very hard to be sociable but longed to be alone.

Sandra, at that time, lived on the outskirts of Dijon (which was quite near Beaune) with a rich, elderly woman. After saying our

JAN
FEB
MAR
APR
MAY
JUNE
JULY
AUG
SEPT
OCT
NOV
DEC

good-byes to our friends we made our way to Sandra's house where the old lady made quite a fuss, clucking like a hen, as she welcomed us in. It was late and we were tired but I did detect a restlessness in Sandra. Our host showed me to a pleasant room with shutters on the windows and explained that the adjacent toilet was temperamental and that I should be careful! I heard Sandra undressing in the room next to me, and strangely, I felt her presence there with me.

My room grew chilly with the night air so I settled into my bed. A restless sleep followed, despite my fatigue. I was rudely awakened by the morning chorus of wild birds as bright beams of sunlight filtered through the cracks in the shutters. Wide awake, I decided to savour the fresh country air.

The house was silent as I crept quietly to the front door. For some reason I wished to see Sandra sleeping. I slowly and very quietly opened her door not wanting to disturb her. There she lay, oblivious to my intrusion, I bent over and breathed in her sleeping breath, lips almost touching, and gently touched her hair. She smiled in her sleep.

My walk in the morning dawn was exhilarating, as life breathed into the Burgundy countryside. I knew that something was happening here, I felt excited and restless. Returning from my walk, the two ladies greeted me with freshly brewed coffee and freshly baked croissants that had been delivered to the doorstep!

We explored Dijon and the surrounding countryside that day. I vividly remember her wearing a long gypsy-style red polka dot skirt, which to enable her to drive had to be hitched up over her knees. We toured the almost mediaeval countryside with little evidence of agricultural activity in its unfenced green rolling fields. The sun beamed down, warm, but as yet not oppressively hot. All day we talked and strolled then dined that evening in Dijon. Our appetites were intensified with the country air and sunshine.

We stumbled, out of the restaurant, into a torrent of early summer rain. Passing an old university building, the sound of piano music lifted through the steamy air. We were completely soaked by this time, but not cold, and we came together in an embrace that lasted and lasted, lifting us into a dreamlike stupor, oblivious of our surroundings.

The rain persisted the next day but did not dampen Sandra's enthusiasm for a horse trek through the dripping mossy Burgundy forests followed by lunch in a tiny country restaurant packed with locals who drank heartily. I was completely famished and devoured an enormous beef bourguignon, the bacon of which had recently been smoked over an open fire. We became quite tipsy, but the sun had now come out, and we went for a walk in the nearby rolling fields to dry out our sodden clothes.

Many wild summer flowers had blossomed, the old oak trees overhead were in full shimmering leaf. A herd of nearby cattle showed a moment's curiosity, much to Sandra's anxiety, until I reassured her of our safety. On the perimeter of this gently undulating summer field, surrounded by wild flowers, we lay down together, as the warm summer breeze whispered through the leaves of the nearby oaks. Rolling over and over in the damp aromatic grass, we both realised that something very special was in the air!

Reluctantly, I had to return home the next day. Like the beginning of my visit, this was to prove equally chaotic. I decided to drive Sandra's car back to Paris, but only left about an hour before my flight was due to depart. 'Faster', she urged. We arrived at the airport with 15 minutes to go. The car screeched to a halt, and like bank robbers the two desperadoes dashed out. A bored crowd waiting for taxis were intrigued by our antics. She hugged and kissed as her eyes streamed with tears. We parted.

I rushed to book in but economy class was now full . . . would I mind an upgrade? Thank you British Airways, a glass of ice-cold champagne was offered as I took my seat. Panting and oozing perspiration, heart thumping, I received chilling stares from fellow businessmen. Oh dear, my life was about to change dramatically, I thought, and smiled warmly to myself as the aircraft accelerated for take-off.

The following months drained each other's bank balances as

JAN
FEB
MAR
APR
MAY
JUNE
JULY
AUG
SEPT
OCT
NOV
DEC

we travelled back and forth from France to Scotland and from Scotland to France. It made no economic sense, but then these things never do! Sandra loved the desolate west-coast landscapes, open deserted beaches, ruins of ancient castles, cosy pubs and bitter beers, accents and kilts, the energetic and pretty cities of Glasgow and Edinburgh, the simple fresh seafood, Italian ice cream, August heather, cheddar cheese and oatcakes on picnics washed down with light wine or whisky topped up with peaty water, the folk music of Capercaillie, and after much coaxing, a vindaloo!

A few months later she invited me to a wine festival in Burgundy, held in the beautiful Celler Musèe Grevin. This is an annual event held since the early 17th century, whereby wine makers come together with the best bottles from their cellars. These are judged by the Chevaliers du Tastevin — the Knights of the Wine Cup who dress in red robes with gold frocks and cardinal-like hats. Their endorsement means a great deal and the occasion is taken very seriously by all taking part. The Tastevin (pronounced taat-ev-an) is a little silver tasting cup similar to our Scottish quaich. Since the early 17th century every self-respecting Burgundy wine grower owned one. The decoration was developed for practical reasons. To best analyse the wine's bouquet the cup opens out like a scallop shell helping the eye to judge colour and leaving plenty of room for a flaring nose to breathe in the heavy scent — a reminder that tasting wine, like indeed malt whisky, begins not at the mouth, but with the eyes and nose.

The reason for my invitation was perhaps, I thought, as consolation in missing the chateaux tour a few months earlier. I for one have very little experience of Burgundy wines, except that I love their white Montrachet which has become outrageously expensive.

Taking the TGV from Paris, I arrived in Dijon at around eight in the evening. It was late autumn now and the leaves on the vines were falling in bronze, copper and magenta hues as the night air grew cooler. Mistletoe nestled in nearby elms, ripening for Christmas. Sandra met me at the station, it was lovely to see her, as the monthly meetings were beginning to take their toll.

The event we were attending was organised by the local Chambre de Commerce comprising mainly of wine makers, hoteliers and restaurateurs. Around 150 attended.

Sandra had, yet again, been over-optimistic in securing me an invitation. As part of the organising committee she had presumed that I could easily be sneaked in. As often as not, at such events, you get a certain amount of 'no shows'! Empty seats look bad, therefore an 'unofficial topping up' is accepted. She struggled to find a suitable name card describing my occupation. Knowing my limited grasp of the French language she excelled by being completely economic with the truth.

My title was freelance food and drink writer — from England! Huh, what a joke with my Scottish accent! Little did she realise, this was to rebound horribly. The vineyard and hotel bosses got wind of my 'presence'. We were invited to the top table, I could have killed her, but it served us bloody well right!

I was studied constantly by watchful eyes, curious about my note making. I believe every morsel and sticky gulp that night was well earned. It was like being in one of those nightmares, when you can't run, the difference being I could not simply wake up. This went on for hours and I cannot believe that the deception went undetected. I thought I had performed well in this tortuous position, commenting constantly on colour, nose and taste. They must have put my ignorance down to British gibberish. For once my poor French helped as it gave me lots of time to consider my answers. On concluding the evening, they asked me when an article would be forthcoming. I gingerly replied, 'In the not too distant future!' Feeling like a pair of cads we skulked away.

If this little story is ever read by the 'Dukes of Burgundy' then let me say this:

'I wholeheartedly apologise'.

If in writing this chapter readers are hopefully encouraged to visit this beautiful part of France, sample its gorgeous food and delicious wines, live in its splendid hostelries, then perhaps, just perhaps I earned my supper that terrifying night! I also offer a

JAN
FEB
MAR
APR
MAY
JUNE
JULY
AUG
SEPT
OCT
NOV
DEC

whisky tasting in return and if I am ever invited back I will bring my best bottle of malt!

In visiting Burgundy of course, readers might also find 'something in the air'!

Is Santa Teetotal?

Many distilleries close down for the festive period. It is perhaps accepted that this is a time to enjoy the product rather than just produce it. Another suggested reason being that 'misjudgements' have been known to occur during this period, the 'funny season'! Perhaps the following story will illustrate my point

It was in 1977 that a new Health and Safety Act came into force in Britain. This Act marked the end of an era for distillery workers in Scotland. The 'free dram' was abolished, an unwelcome decision. For years a large dram of over-proof whisky was administered to warehousemen, mashmen and stillmen alike at the beginning and end of a shift. This was either a 'brown dram' (matured) or 'spike' (new whisky spirit). There was also the 'dirty work' dram, for example for cleaning out the boiler tubes. It was a strong tradition and especially well received during the harsh winter months.

I have mixed feelings about this change. True, many now travel to work by car whereas in the old days houses were provided on site, so tottering home, inebriated, endangered no one! Even today, French wine pickers are allowed generous samples of their products, after their sweaty, back-breaking work. Distillery workers do, however receive one bottle a month, but there must have been some cases of severe withdrawal symptoms. I suppose in the name of safety the Act is sensible and reduces the chances of accidents and mistakes occurring.

Talking of mistakes, a particular incident comes to mind. It concerned a distillery, near Elgin, with a rather large mash tun. At

JAN
FEB
MAR
APR
MAY
JUNE
JULY
AUG
SEPT
OCT
NOV
DEC

75

the that time, many moons ago, I was employed as a stillman by another whisky company and was involved in one such incident which is worth relating again. This vessel, about the size and volume of a large living room, is used to extract the sugars from the grist (the ground malted barley), acting a bit like a huge tea strainer. When full it holds 65,000 litres and 18 tonnes of grist, in a sweet porridge-like consistency. The base of this huge vessel has four portholes, opened with the aid of screws, for the removal of drained grist. There is usually an awaiting truck below to capture this. Now these portholes are activated, on the mashman's

control console, by simply turning a key. At the beginning of each shift and before filling the mash tun, the port doors are checked, and when they are securely closed, the key is removed and kept in the mash-man's pocket.

One year a catastrophe took place nine days before Christmas. A colleague, a mash-man, who will remain nameless, had received a particularly large measure that night which topped up his daytime intake. His big mistake was not remembering to remove the key at the beginning of his shift. Around 2.00am a very distressed mashman came rushing through to the still house where I was working. 'Malcolm, come quickly and bring a bucket and shovel', he implored, his eyes bloodshot and stricken with terror. He had accidentally knocked the key that was still in place, unaware of this he left for his tea break. Meanwhile, the portholes mercilessly opened up and its contents oozed out. We were met by a horrific scene. The truck was unrecognisable, enveloped by a hot gungy-porridge. A river of the stuff was creeping like volcanic lava towards the manager's office.

'Quick', he shouted, 'start shovelling!'

'To where?', I cried in despair. It was a hopeless gesture, all the pumps were now out of action. There was another problem. Mr Mashman had half-filled the fermentation vats (washbacks) and added yeast to ferment in full vats. Of course now there was no more, as the mashtun was now empty. In effect, the supper for these active yeasty organisms had a main course, but no pudding. These tiny mites were starting to go berserk as froth poured over the top of the vats.

'Help, help', wailed the mashman. 'What will we do?'

We? I thought.

It was now 4.00am and he reluctantly called the brewer. 'This had better be important', responded the brewer.

'Kind of', came the timid reply.

It took three days to clean up the mess. Mr Mashman was lucky and was sent to the 'close'. (A term used for working on 'general duties' around the distillery).

One of my final Christmas 'duties' as a salesman was to visit one of our best London customers, Milroy's whisky shop in Greek Street, Soho. The brothers Jack and Wallace Milroy are undoubtedly legendary whisky characters and raconteurs. These larger than life gentlemen sport unequalled stamina, are infinitely

JAN
FEB
MAR
APR
MAY
JUNE
JULY
AUG
SEPT
OCT
NOV
DEC

77

knowledgeable and incessantly sociable. They are a blessing to the Scotch whisky industry. Wallace was the first to recognise the burgeoning interest in malts among the public and wrote his *Malt Whisky Almanac* in 1986, an unbiased directory of distilleries and malts which has inspired many other writers to follow suit. In the six editions to date it has sold over 250,000 copies worldwide and I highly recommend it.

On each visit, an opened bottle would appear from under the counter, always something new or a little bit different. Customers were encouraged to sample and experience new bottlings, which was fascinating to watch. Special guests were often invited downstairs to a tasting cellar. Some have been known to regret this move, that is if they managed to survive having lunch with the brothers. This is a novel experience that takes place in a little known Chinese restaurant in Soho. Jack's favourite ploy is to ask if you would like to sample his woman? 'She is kept in the back room,' he explains. A knowing look to the waiter prompts him to return with a decanter shaped into the most gorgeous, curved female form, which contains the most delicious whisky. It's late in the afternoon, and my flight to Inverness leaves in one and a half hours. I start making blurred calculations of tube times . . . Piccadilly line to Heathrow . . . check-in . . .

' . . . have another dram!', booms Jack.

After a long year's production of whisky and with the first fall of snow the holidays begin in earnest with the staff Christmas lunch. The party is held 'in house' at the distillery reception centre. With our party hats on we pull crackers, tell bad jokes, exchange presents and drink and make merry. Filled with 'the Christmas spirit' I began to think of the ten million litres of Glenfarclas malt whisky in the nearby cellars. Now that would make a serious party! This is where I would head should a nuclear war ever break out. Mind you, a three minute warning does not give you much time. In any event I would have a bloody good try!

It is a long-standing tradition for the owner to signal the start of the festivities. John Grant performs a masterful piece of swordsmanship. With sabre in hand he cleanly slices the top off a champagne bottle and its contents are quickly consumed by the revellers. The day ends in a fuggy-haze at the local Aberlour Hotel. The company is like a close-knit family so the team mingle in the relaxed festive atmosphere: non-smokers smoke, someone slides off a chair, a rude joke is shared, the barriers are lowered, a wanton cuddle here and a smooch there. A great day out!

And lastly on this wonderful subject of Christmas I was sitting in O'Malley's Irish Bar in Helsinki a few months previously when I met a dark-haired lady by the name of Tuula Korhonen. She was as dark as the Guinness in front of me. Tuula, like many other Finnish ladies, takes ice in her beer. I thought they might have seen enough of the stuff — Lapland being only 200 miles north on the Arctic Circle.

I introduced her to malt whisky, but our brand was not in this bar . . . yet. The young drinkers here are still possessed by vodka. I explained that a great deal of whisky was drunk by all ages in

JAN
FEB
MAR
APR
MAY
JUNE
JULY
AUG
SEPT
OCT
NOV
DEC

Scotland and that new consumers were being targeted by advertising campaigns. During the course of our conversation we began to discuss Santa Claus. Tuula explained that Santa was definitely Finnish. Christmas trees may have German origins, St Nicholas might be Dutch but Santa was 100 per cent Finnish! She told me he lives in Korva-Tunduri with his wife Maija and their many offspring. She added that he was a pillar of respectability, clean-living, teetotal and never seen in Helsinki bars! I argued that I knew differently. She was surprised to hear this and quizzed me some more. I explained that as children on Christmas Eve we always left out a dram of malt whisky and some shortbread on the kitchen table for Santa.

The glass was always empty in the morning!

Merry Christmas and may your God go with you!

Malt Whisky Tasting –
INFORMATIVE, INTERESTING & FUN

GETTING STARTED

Anyone with a reasonable grasp of simple chemistry, a basic grounding in Scotch whisky, a little knowledge of the regional styles, but most importantly who appreciates things that smell and taste good, can very comfortably and confidently make a good presentation.

You do not need to be a public speaker or a comedian, a little humour is, however, highly recommended. Just be yourself — but be prepared!

I suggest that the presenter keeps the 'tasting' short and sweet (45 minutes) with a time for questions at the end. Tests have proven that the peak concentration span for medical students is around 30 minutes. So watch your time!

Also remember that no tasting should be conducted in the manner of a glass of whisky being thrust into someone's hand with a sales rep spouting that this is the 'best in the world', that does not work anymore. Consumers are much more discerning than they often appear.

TO WHOM?

Many whisky appreciation societies, academies and clubs are mushrooming up all over the world. The question therefore has to be asked, to whom is the presentation going to be made? I have tried to categorise these as:

A. *Novices*
With little or no knowledge of whisky, who perhaps have tasted something less than marvellous but still are willing to try something new with perhaps a fashionable and chic value.

B. *Intermediates*
Those who have a reasonable knowledge and appreciate malt whisky, often they are brand loyal.

C. *Connoisseurs and experts*
Those who have many years of experience, have attended many tastings and tours and are well read in whisky literature.

By far the most common group is A, followed by B. Type C is still rare and confined mainly to the trade and journalists. In the latter case the tasting would be more detailed and gauged towards their knowledge, perhaps concentrating on the importance of wood in the maturation of whisky. That besides, these notes are aimed specifically at groups A and B.

WHERE? CHOICE OF VENUE
I never feel comfortable with modern, bright, airy auditoriums, with a plinth, microphone and a sea of unknown faces. This is definitely the wrong environment!

I would suggest a low ceiling, cellar-style environment with small tables accommodating 4-6 persons each. Comfortably lit, a log fire is ideal. Some restaurants lend themselves to this ambience, as do many good pubs. I have not tried a Caribbean beach bar yet, but am open to persuasion!

Seriously though, the location is of great importance and helps enormously in the success of the event. Avoid lecturing at all costs! Keep the group size under 25 people; 40 maximum (the larger the group, the shyer the individual) and try to mingle, always encouraging an exchange of views. Remember tastings are highly individual, people will experience different things, but more on this later.

Lastly the 'feel good factor' is important, it is supposed to be an enjoyable event and many are paying for the privilege!

THE 'ESSENTIAL BIT'
1. *Malt Whisky — Choosing Malts & Regional Tasting*
I am essentially biased, having been raised in Speyside. This is malt whisky country where the homes of the major brands are located. No whisky tasting would be complete without a good Speyside. Colleagues in France from Bordeaux and Burgundy suffer this same malady and like the spoiled brats that we undoubtedly are, often over-emphasise regional favourites. Try to avoid this, as often as not in sampling regional varieties, a Speyside will often 'shine through'.

I suggest therefore a good Speyside, 10-year-old Glenfarclas single malt. Ideal.

An Islay — Lagavulin or Bowmore 10-year-old single malt.

A Campbeltown — Springbank 10-year-old single malt. Possibly something not specific to generic regional location e.g. Talisker from Skye, Glenmorangie from Tain or Highland Park from Orkney. Perhaps a blend such as Bell's 8-year-old or Isle of Skye. (This helps explain the differences between malt and blended whisky. Allow one bottle per 25 tasters).

VERTICAL TASTING ONE BRAND
It is usual for me to use Glenfarclas malt whisky for tasting . . . no surprises there! The most common method is to sample a range of ages and strengths (to include 105° cask strength). Glenfarclas is ideal for this and for a straightforward tasting the 10-year-old, 15-year-old, 25-year-old and the '105' fit the bill.

Unlike wine, the production of new whisky 'spirit' is little if at all affected by inclement weather. A particularly hot or wet summer may affect the supply of local malted barley but quality malted barley is now traded Euro and world-wide so this raw ingredient is always abundant at good quality.

Methods of production are essentially similar from distillery to distillery. I am not an advocate to the tune that a dent in a process pipe is essential to the character of the final product. No, the short birth of new spirit (three days) is indeed critical, the skills of the stillman paramount in avoiding feinty unwanted 'cuts', but essential to the new whisky will be its upbringing to maturity. Like humans, maturity is reached at varying ages and under different conditions. It is therefore an essential point to be made during any discussion or tasting that the role of the cask/barrel is not understated. More on this later.

Let us progress: having selected either a regional grouping of malts, or a single malt of differing ages, we must decide on our format. I recommend the following procedure.

2. *Water*

As water is one, if not the single most determining factor in a malt whisky, it is essential that you choose a good quality, Scottish, still water. Bottled in glass, Highland Spring water is ideal. Do not stint on this and avoid highly chlorinised city waters at all costs. Some in your group may baulk at the thought of adding anything to their cherished whisky but explain that a little splash of good water does in fact help to release hidden aromas and has been described as similar to the effect of rainwater in aiding a flower to open fully and release its full bouquet.

The water and whisky should be at room temperature, never too hot or too cold. Adding ice to malt whisky seriously reduces its bouquet, something you are paying for!

You can be excused however if you fancy a long tall drink on a hot day! These little points can be expressed during your tasting.

GLASSES

Scrupulously clean fluted glasses with stems are ideal, forget the cut crystal, they look nice but are quite inappropriate. You need something you can get your nose into!

Cognac glasses are ideal but white wine flutes will suffice. Never use brand new ex-factory glasses until they have been washed thoroughly. John Lamond, The Master of the Malt and author of *The Malt File*, takes this further — he always hand polishes each glass to get rid of any cardboard smells or residue — that's what I call professional!

When pouring your samples for nosing and tasting, one centimetre of whisky is enough, with just a splash of water.

MY PROPS

We now have the group in front of us, seated, comfortable and ready to go. The samples are in front of them, water is at hand.

Introduce yourself and then follow by explaining the reason for your interest in malt whisky. It may simply be you like a certain taste or find the whole subject fascinating, or you just want to learn more.

Explain what is in front of the group, i.e. regional malts and describe roughly the region such as Islay, West Coast or Scottish island 'blasted by the Atlantic'. A poster of Scotland helps enormously when doing this.

For myself I usually describe a little about the distillery, its history, methods of production, major markets and special attributes.

BRINGING THE DISTILLERY TO THEM

It is often said that the best place for a whisky tasting is a distillery. That is true, but not always possible! To begin describing the process of distilling without the distillery atmosphere will I suggest, send many to sleep. Keep this part simple. This is what I do.

1. To explain malting and malted barley I usually have a small bag of malted barley which is passed round the group, they can crunch it to experience the sweet sugars achieved through germination. Most distilleries will send samples of malted barley for this purpose.

2. I use a mortar and pestle to describe the milling of the malted barley. To explain how the mash tun works to extract the sugars, a French cafetière is ideal. Simply pour hot (not boiling) water

over your ground barley and push down the strainer and there you have a sweet liquor, which smells and tastes malty and is very pleasant. This can be passed round safely.

PEAT

I always carry pieces of peat turf to help explain:
1. The effect this material has on water — its sponge-like characteristics.
2. Its smoky aromatic effect on drying malted barley.
(A recent tasting by Jonas Wahlman in Stockholm last year amazed me! He allowed small pieces of peat to smoulder gently during the tasting, which greatly enhanced the atmosphere. But remember to douse with water afterwards, and never do this near smoke detectors!)

DISTILLING METHODS OF PRODUCTION

It has been said that if you can boil a kettle, then you can make whisky. This is an oversimplification, yes the process is essentially simple, but it is often quite difficult to convey to a group.

By this time the cafetière will have made its rounds. Explain that if yeast is added to that liquid then fermentation will take place. After two days a beery brew ready for distillation will exist. Crack open a malty beer, pour into a glass, explain that a beer similar to this is then distilled. Take a gulp . . . you get thirsty talking!

If there is an electric kettle (cold) at hand, explain that essentially a pot still acts in a similar manner. Heated either directly from below or via a coil inside.

Explain quickly that if the beer was boiled gently in that kettle (do not do this physically) and that if the resultant steam vapour could be cooled to form condensate then simple distilling would be occurring.

Explain that if you did all this now, you would probably be arrested — that usually gets a laugh!

You may think that I am skipping through these procedures in a flippant manner but remember that these details can only be emulated crudely away from an actual distillery. It is better to concentrate on aspects which are pro-active with the group.

THE TASTING

By this time 15 minutes will have elapsed. As the evening is supposed to be pleasurable as well as informative, it is now time to get 'into' that first dram.

	10 YEAR OLD	'105'CASK STRENGTH	21 YEAR OLD
COLOUR	Straw with good gold highlights.	Deep peaty amber with gold highlights.	Antique amber.
NOSE	Delicately sweet, leafy oak with a coffee tang.	Spirity yet sweet.	Full complex notes of rich, sweet malt.
TASTE	Sweet, malty, full rich and round.	Spirity, malty, a little oily-oak character.	Oak, juicy fruit, vanilla.
FINISH	Slightly spicy, long and characterful.	Long, dry and flavoursome.	Smoky aroma with a long lingering finish.

Explain and describe the first sample, its age and location. How you would savour whisky. Ask people in the group how they would describe the following attributes. Colour, nose, taste and finish.

I have filled in a few to give you the idea. Incidentally, professional tasters do not actually taste, they rely totally on their 'nose' often using coloured blue nosing glasses to reduce the effect of their eyes leading or confusing their sense of smell. Because of the alcoholic strength the tasting sensation is reduced as you sample further malts or ages. You can still however detect differences in nose and flavour.

WATER

Explain the importance of water. Pure spring water often filters down through peat and over limestone or granite, taking an imprint from the local landscape, as unique as the regional soils of France. This is a huge determining feature to the end result, affected by weather and geography, proximity to the sea and local geological detail. It is impossible to emulate in a laboratory. The masters of innovation, the Japanese, having simply ceased trying and have instead bought over quality Scottish distilleries such as Tomatin, Bowmore and Macallan.

MICRO-CLIMATE

The micro-climate, like the source of water, plays an essential role. Barrels matured away from the 'mother' distillery rarely have the same quality aspirations as those matured at home, something which dumbfounds scientists and chemists alike.

The very 'air' the cask 'breathes' is therefore unique to each distillery's location. Witness the result of Islay malts taking in lungfuls of salty Atlantic sea fogs, compared to the freezing frosty Highland winters with their often moist balmy summers. These are the truly magical features of the great malts.

WOOD

The upbringing of the newly produced whisky is essential. Care and attention is critical, as is the selection of good wood. Oak is perfect — hard yet porous. It lets very little out, but a great deal in! In explaining the importance of wood I usually pass round an oak stave (a section of cask) from a barrel which has usually stored sherry previously. Many old casks are broken up after use, but continue to exude wonderful aromas. You can enhance this by rubbing a little whisky into the grain of the wood! Spanish oak casks from Seville and Jerez which have stored sherry previously are much sought after. Some companies are experimenting with port and Madeira wood as alternatives. Perhaps it was by pure chance that the industry caught on to the attributes of sherry wood many years ago.

I do not know of a plausible explanation, other than that a good sherry barrel helps enormously in producing a characterful whisky. It helps to develop colour, nose and taste.

TIME

The length of maturation of fine malt whisky is unique to each brand. The age statement on the product is a quality statement. The distiller is stating the number of years that whisky has been matured in bond. Avoid vague diluted age statements like 'fine old vintage' or 'very special reserve'. These are marketeers' jargon.

An age statement is a malt's pedigree. Without such, it's like buying a car without a log book and mileage record.

Remember also that the distiller by law, when expressing an age statement, is stipulating the youngest age of any product in that bottle. However, an eye drop of 10-year-old whisky is not added to 99.9% of the contents of a three-year-old product. The contents of a 10-year-old malt are likely to contain substantially older malts to bring the product 'up' to the distiller's stringent evaluation of what is considered a marketable product.

By now the evening is coming to a close, your group should be 'relaxed' by now, with the 'feel good' factor high.

You will note that I do not use videos or a slide projector. Personally I find these very passive ways of communicating, but some may find such equipment of use.

ROUNDING OFF

I usually break off by saying that this is the end of the whisky tasting and offer a short period on questions. Very often a question will be raised to which you do not know the answer. I suggest you carry a few reference books to aid this purpose. Remember that malt whisky, its culture, history and future will conjure up many unanswerable questions — do not worry too much about this.

Be as truthful as possible and answer as 'you' see fit. Never profess to be an expert.

Finally, I try to make the point that malt whisky is a highly individual thing and that some of the group will understandably have derived more satisfaction than others.

Some will have experienced different sensations to their senses of smell and taste. This is the magic of malt whisky tasting. (I once read a description which colourfully described the product as follows: 'Like the fragrance of Scottish bogland mist rising on a summer morn.')

At a recent tasting I asked two separate 'nosers' to close their eyes and try to explain what they were smelling. One commented that the malt was 'like Christmas cake' and the other 'like an old Barbour wax jacket'. Individual responses! That is the fun and joy of whisky tasting.

These notes are only intended as a rough guide in the hope that your tasting is enjoyable and rewarding.

TASTINGS TO GROUP C
(Connoisseurs and experts)

I have described this group as those who have many years of experience, have attended many tastings and distillery tours and are well read in whisky literature.

This can be a daunting prospect, even to someone with many years experience. On these occasions I believe it is essential that you ask the distillery for assistance. This is normally well received, but requires plenty of lead time.

Group C will already know the fundamentals of malting, fermentation, distilling and maturation. They will also know whisky culture and will have tasted the major regional brands.

My advice would be to concentrate on a specific and essential part of malt whisky production or marketing. The importance of good wood is one aspect we at Glenfarclas particularly concentrate on. We can truthfully say, hand on heart, that we take no shortcuts on this.

The effects of wood on new spirit can be described best with the assistance of samples, often drawn from casks.

TO START: FOR NOSING ONLY

1. **New spirit**: the group will pass around several samples and nose the result. New spirit, colourless, is often described as being spirity yet with sweet overtones. From this point you can then develop the argument for maturation in good wood.

2. **Plain wood sample**: 8 year old. A sample passed around will show the softening and rounding effects of a plain oak cask giving a little colour (light straw) but also an important balance to the final product. Not overpowering or dominating, yet still helps the micro-climate to influence the flavour.

3. **Sherry cask**: 8 year old. Samples passed round will indicate the colour and taste influences of such casks. These create the delightful rich dark brown ambers which are a delight to the eye.

Sherry wood however does produce some very powerful aromas often described as being vanilla, chocolate and fruity in character. These are wonderful additions to the body of a good malt, but should never dominate it. Further explain that these two types of cask are essential in producing a well-balanced malt. Samples of staves can also be passed round the group.

For the tasting I suggest using one very youthful malt followed by something special and older — perhaps a 30-year-old Glenfarclas, or, as is popular in Germany, a single cask, single vintage bottling.

Most of the previous points aimed at groups A & B can be reiterated, for example, the importance of the age statement, use of good water etc. Quality brochures and literature should accompany such presentations. Rarely do groups like these exceed more than 15 persons. You do however have to offer much more detail, so do liaise with the distillery or distributor/wholesaler.

Lastly a note to distributors abroad.

Essential as they are, overseas trips are expensive and time consuming. One aspect I feel which is still 'under-developed' is to coincide these marketing meetings with a tasting. These could be targeted towards major customers in the on or off-trade, or simply to the key sales personnel, the latter of which would then know the 'basics' in conducting their own tastings in their own style and language. Tastings are a low cost, yet highly effective way of creating face to face brand loyalty.

Recommended reading:

The Malt Whisky Almanac (6th edition), Wallace Milroy, Neil Wilson Publishing Ltd.

The Malt Whisky File (2nd edition), John D Lamond & Robin Tucek, Canongate Books.

A Taste of Scotch, Derek Cooper, André Deutsch.

A Wee Dram, David Daiches, André Deutsch.

A-Z of Whisky, Gavin D. Smith, Neil Wilson Publishing Ltd.

The Abbey Court Restaurant

15, Greyfriars St
Elgin IV30 1LF

Tel/Fax (01343) 542849
email - abbeycourt@aol.com

Our Fayre

Morning Coffees *** Bar and Snack Lunches
Full À la Carte Luncheon

*   *   *

Bar Suppers *** Blackboard Specials ***
Full À La Carte Dinner Menu

Extensive Wine List & Classic Malt Selection

"A timeless presence in an ever changing world"

Tastefully refurbished to the highest standards, we offer the rare opportunity of savouring the style and elegance of a by-gone era combined with the comforts and service of a first class hotel.

❖ Beautiful individually furnished and decorated en suite bedrooms each with welcome tray, remote control TV, radio, trouser press and hair dryer.
❖ Golfing Breaks, Whisky Weekends, Murder and Mystery Weekends.
❖ Christmas and Hogmanay House Parties.
❖ The Quaich Bar – internationally famous with 200 different Malt Whiskies.
❖ Library, Drawing Room, Games Room, Sauna, Exercise Room, Beauty Salon.
❖ Morning coffees, light lunches, afternoon teas.
❖ 2 AA rosette award winning restaurant using only the finest wild and local produce, individually prepared by our Chefs just for you. (dinner reservations essential)
❖ AA 3 star, STB 4 crown – Highly Commended, Member of the Virgin Hotel Collection, Taste of Scotland, Johansens Recommended Hotels and Scotland's Commended Hotels.

Craigellachie,
Banffshire,
AB38 9SR.

Telephone 01340 881 204   Facsimile 01340 881 253

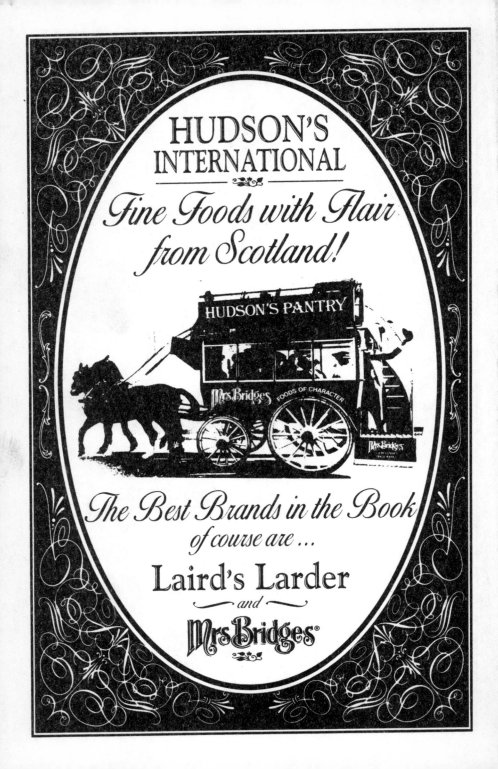

SPEYSIDE COOPERAGE VISITOR CENTRE
DUFFTOWN ROAD, CRAIGELLACHIE,
BANFFSHIRE, SCOTLAND AB38 9RS
TELEPHONE (01340) 871108
FAX (01340) 881303
EXHIBITION - VIEWING GALLERY - GIFT SHOP
WINNER OF NINE MAJOR AWARDS

ISLE OF SKYE
YEAR 8 OLD
BLENDED SCOTCH WHISKY

MARKET LEADER

Perhaps not in the U.K., but certainly in the Starr Inn in Tain where it outsells other blends by about 4 to 1.

Why?

Because Highlanders know quite a bit about whisky. They know that the youngest whisky in this 19th century recipe is 8 years old (the age of a blend being defined as the age of the youngest whisky in that blend).

They know that age produces unrivalled mellowness and smoothness and they also know a bargain when they see one. Because, surprisingly, Isle of Skye is available for the price of an ordinary blend.

Fortunately, you don't have to go as far North as Tain to find a bottle. Simply pop into Sainsbury's or your local independent and you'll find it tucked in amongst it's younger brethren. Unless, of course, you're planning a holiday in the Highlands this year - in which case you'll find it everywhere.

STOCKISTS

UK	Scotland
Savacentre	Asda
Major Sainsbury's	Tesco
Major Budgen's	Victoria Wine
Stewarts Wine	Haddows
Barrel	Scotmid
	Selected Threshers
	Selected Co-ops

AND INDEPENDENT STOCKISTS THROUGHOUT THE COUNTRY

Ian Macleod & Co. 01506 852205 e-mail Ian.Macleod@btinternet.com.

ESTABLISHED 1836

Glenfarclas ®

"...In it is to be found the sunshine and shadow that chased each other over the billowy cornfield, the hum of the bee, and hope of Spring, the breath of May, the carol of the lark, the distant purple of heather in the mountain mist, the dew of the morn, and the wealth of Autumn's rich content all golden with imprisoned light..."

A RIVAL DISTILLER LONDON
May 30th, 1912